RADZI'S INCREDIBLE FACTS

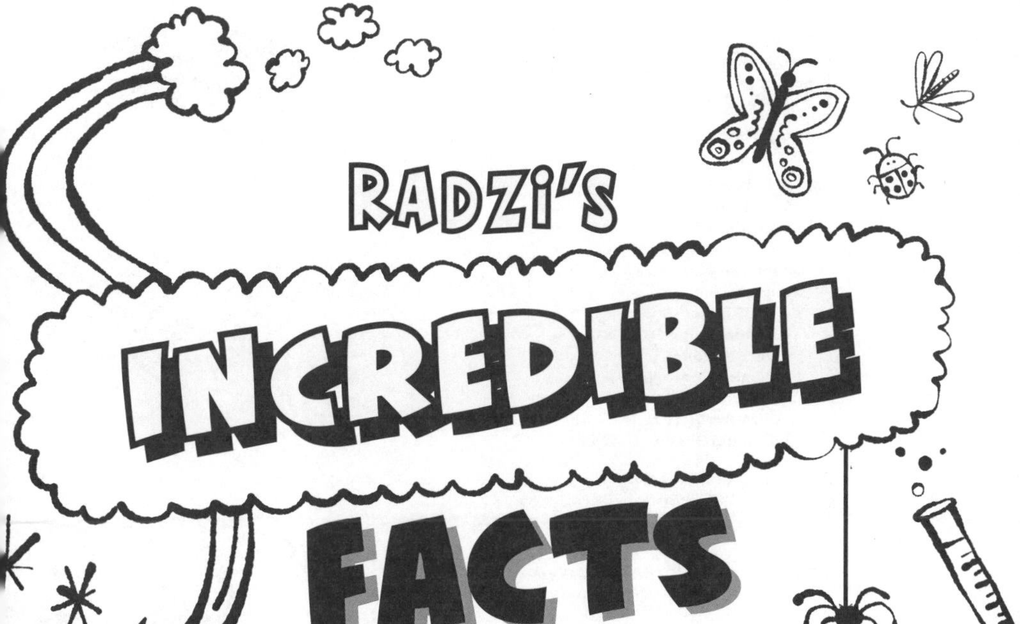

By Radzi Chinyanganya
Illustrations by Laura Wood

Author Radzi Chinyanganya
Illustrator Laura Wood
Acquisitions Editor James Mitchem
Editor Becca Arlington
Senior Designer Rachael Parfitt Hunt
Designers Sif Nørskov, Ann Cannings
US Editor Jill Hamilton
US Senior Editor Shannon Beatty
Production Editor Dragana Puvacic
Production Controller John Casey
Jacket Coordinator Magda Pszuk
Deputy Art Director Mabel Chan
Publishing Director Sarah Larter

First American Edition, 2024
Published in the United States by DK Publishing,
a division of Penguin Random House LLC
1745 Broadway, 20th Floor, New York, NY 10019

24 25 26 27 28 10 9 8 7 6 5 4 3 2 1
001-326997-Feb/2024

Published in Great Britain by Dorling Kindersley Limited

A catalog record for this book
is available from the Library of Congress.
ISBN 978-0-7440-9541-8

DK books are available at special discounts when purchased in bulk for sales promotions, premiums, fund-raising, or educational use.
For details, contact: DK Publishing Special Markets,
1745 Broadway, 20th Floor, New York, NY 10019
SpecialSales@dk.com

Printed and bound in China

www.dk.com

MIX
Paper | Supporting responsible forestry
FSC™ C018179

This book was made with Forest Stewardship Council™ certified paper–one small step in DK's commitment to a sustainable future.
For more information go to www.dk.com/our-green-pledge

CONTENTS

A message from RADZI

I have been a TV presenter for over ten years, and in that time I've been lucky enough to meet some truly incredible people—from the biggest and best people in sports and social media, acting and astronomy, politics and presenting, music and the military, to "ordinary" people with extraordinary stories. But no matter who they are, they all have something fascinating to say!

That's much easier to do when you are an expert, and much harder when you are too young to be one. Besides, you can't be an expert at everything anyway...

Or can you? Can you know something about almost everything, for any conversation you ever have?

A book FULL of AMAZING FACTS

If so, would you need to be good at school subjects? Would you need to be the smartest in your classroom? Thankfully not, because life isn't like school:

Firstly, being good at one subject doesn't mean that you'll be good at another (that's knowing a lot about a little.) Secondly, we don't have tests to prove how much we really know.

In everyday life, how clever you are is actually about how clever you APPEAR. So by simply knowing something small, it will seem as if it's just one of the many things you know. Like in the classroom of life, being the smartest kid is about knowing a little about a lot. That's what learning some of the fascinating facts in this book will help you to achieve! As you'll appear to know something about almost everything!

HUMAN BODY

SPORTS

PLACES

FOOD and DRINK

HISTORY
MUSIC
ANIMALS and NATURE
SCIENCE

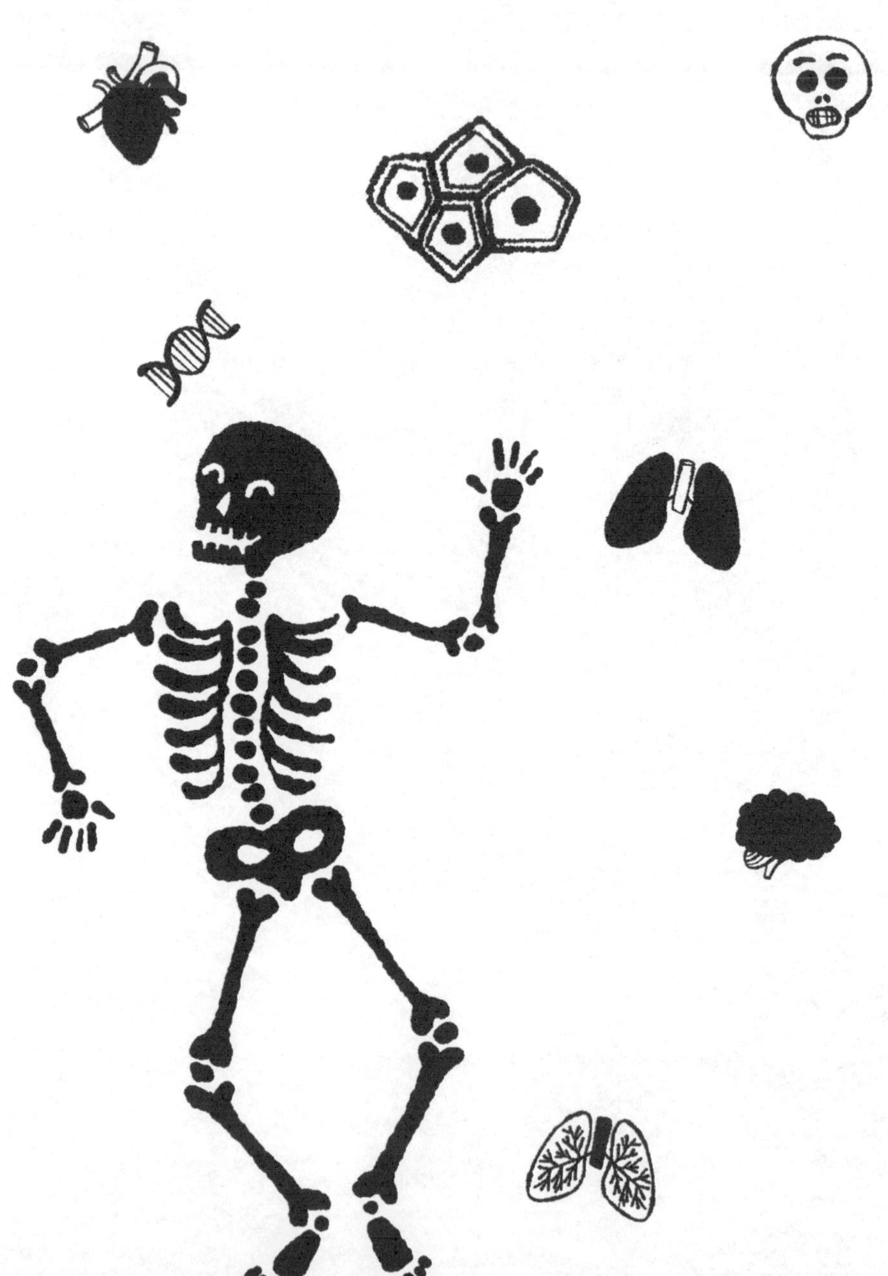

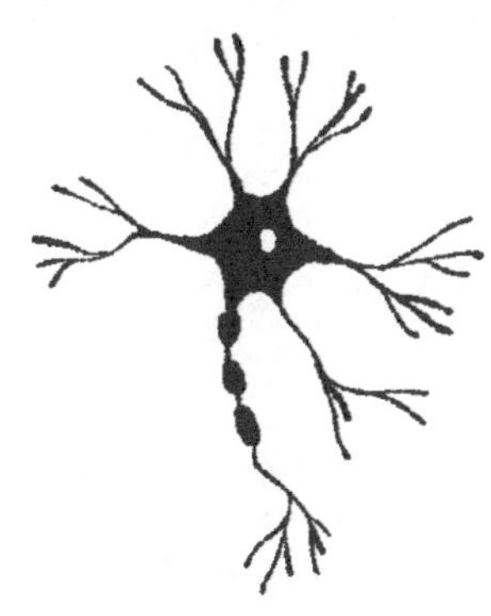

HUMAN BODY

Bonkers BONE FACTS

Arms are one of the most **commonly broken bones**, and they make up nearly half of all adults' broken bones.

We have two types of bone. **Cortical bones** make up 80 percent of our skeleton, and are dense and hard. **Trabecular bones** are softer and spongy, and are found inside large bones, as well as the pelvis, ribs, and skull.

There are **206 bones** in an adult human skeleton. More than half of them are in the hands and feet.

Babies are born with 300 bones.

The **tallest** ever human skeleton belonged to a British man named **Robert Wadlow,** who lived between **1918 and 1940**. He was **8ft 11 inches**.

99 percent of people have **12 ribs**. A small number of people have **13**.

The longest bone in our bodies is the femur, or thigh bone. It's also the strongest.

Teeth are stronger than bones.

The only bone that isn't connected to another bone is the hyoid bone in our throat. It holds our tongue in place.

The smallest bone in the human body is the stapes. It's a tiny bone in the inner ear.

Brilliant BRAIN FACTS

The brain is one of the most **complex** and fascinating organs in our bodies, and its **storage** capacity is considered virtually **unlimited**.

A piece of **brain tissue** the size of a **grain of sand** contains **100,000** neurons and **1 billion** synapses.

Information in the brain travels up to **268 mph** (**431 kmh**).

The human brain consists of about 86 billion neurons. Each neuron forms connections to other neurons, which could add up to 1 quadrillion (written as 1,000,000,000,000,000!) connections. Over time, these neurons can combine, increasing storage capacity.

60 percent of the human brain is made of **fat**. These fatty acids are crucial for the brain's **performance**.

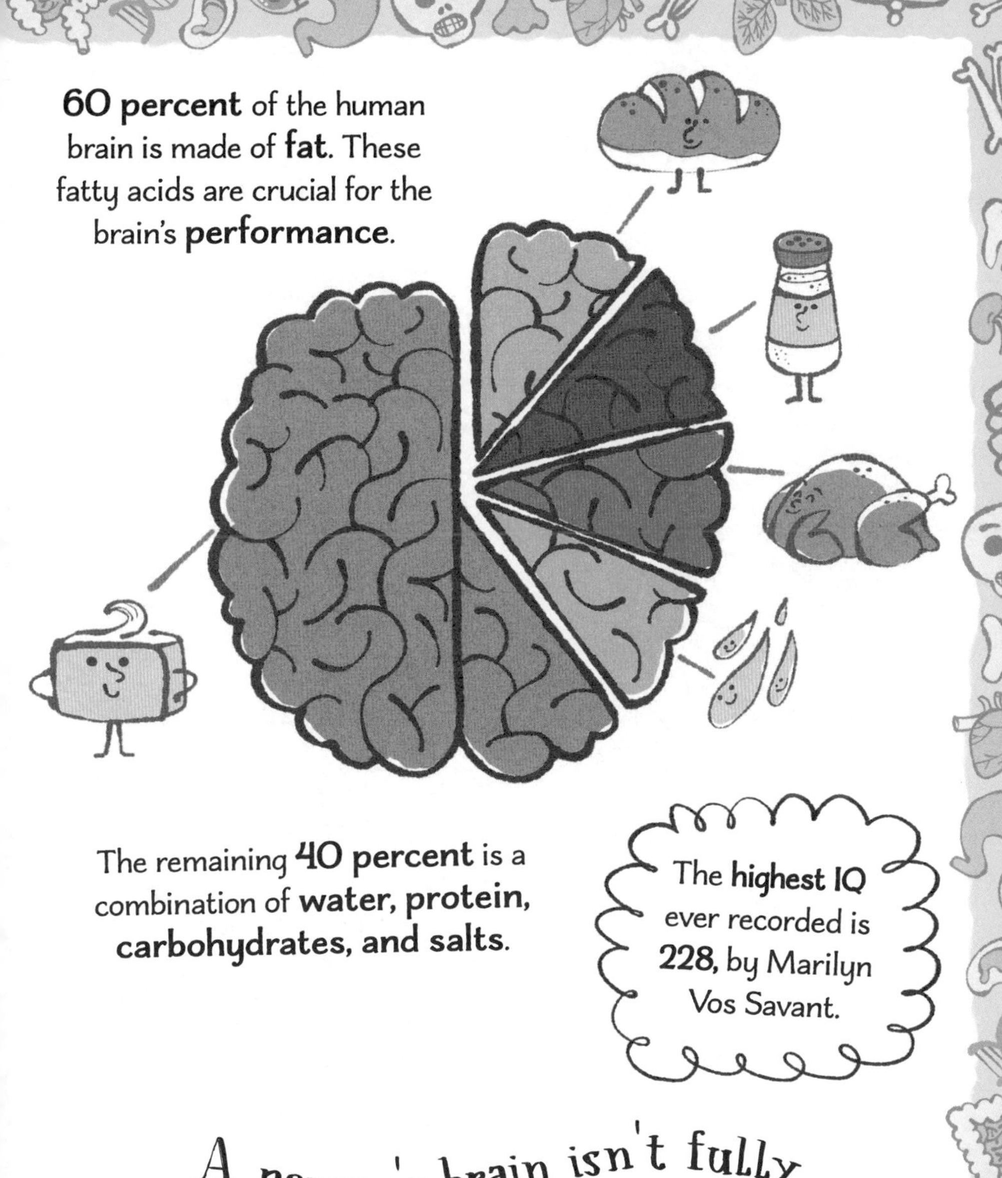

The remaining **40 percent** is a combination of **water, protein, carbohydrates, and salts.**

The **highest IQ** ever recorded is **228,** by Marilyn Vos Savant.

A person's brain isn't fully formed until they're 25 years old.

Smart HEART FACTS

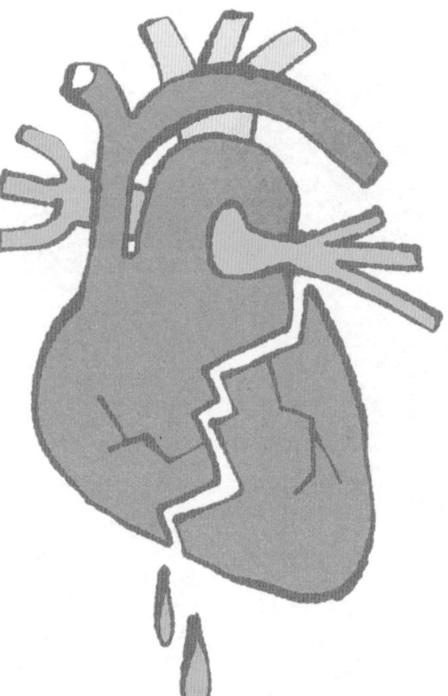

Our hearts have their own **electrical supply**, and still beat even if they're separated from our bodies.

The sound of a heartbeat is the clap of the valves opening and closing.

Human hearts beat over 100,000 times per day.

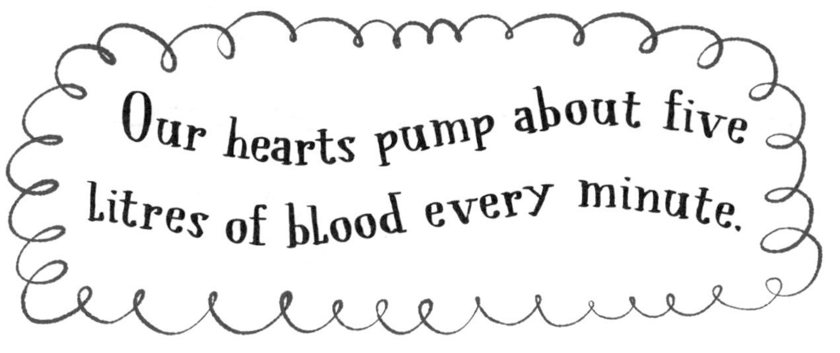

People really can have a **broken heart**—some situations can cause temporary **heart failure**.

Our **hearts** pump **blood** to every cell in our bodies (apart from the **corneas in our eyes**).

Women's hearts beat faster than men's...on average **eight times more per minute**.

The **lowest resting heartbeat** on record is **27 bpm**. The record holder is **Martin Brady**, a British man born in **1969**.

Lots of LUNG FACTS

The **Left Lung** tends to be **smaller** than the **right Lung** to accommodate for the **heart**, which is located on the left side of the body.

A person usually breathes an average of 13 pints (7.4 liters) of air every minute.

Most people only breathe through one nostril at a time. Some people notice that nostril switches at sunrise and sunset!

GB Olympic rowing champion Peter Reed has the highest known lung capacity of any human, at **20.5 pints (11.7 liters)**.

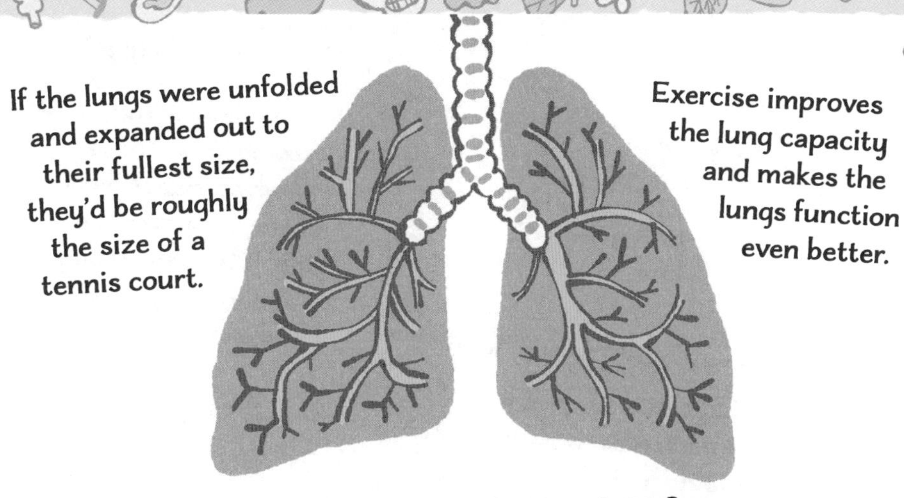

If the lungs were unfolded and expanded out to their fullest size, they'd be roughly the size of a tennis court.

Exercise improves the lung capacity and makes the lungs function even better.

Lungs can float on water and are the only organ that can.

The **lung capacity** of an **adult** is about **eight to twelve pints of air. Males** tend to have larger lung capacity than **females.**

Coughing isn't always bad for our lungs, as it clears our airways.

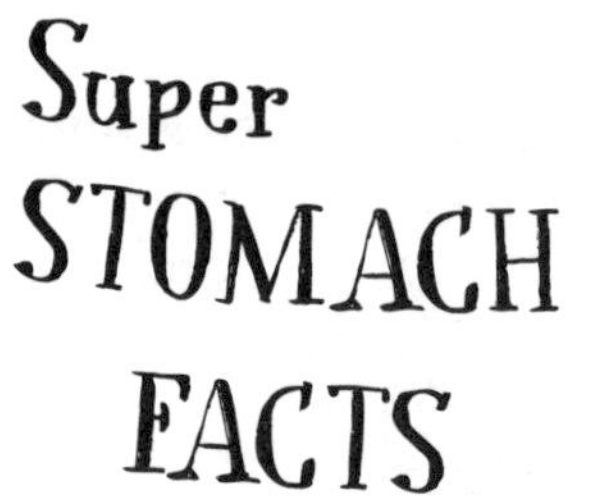

The acid in our stomach is strong enough to digest most of the organs in the body. It is even strong enough to **dissolve** some **metals**!

A human could survive if their stomach was **removed**; they would just need to alter their diet and eat frequent, but smaller, meals.

It takes around **six to eight hours** for food to pass through the **stomach** and into the **intestine**. It can also take up to **three days** for food to travel from being chewed in our **mouths** to entering the **toilet**!

Burping releases **air molecules** that have been **consumed** along with **food** from the **digestive tract.**

When empty, the stomach is pretty small (about the size of a fist). However, it is also capable of stretching to hold up to 7 pints (4 liters) of food, which is the equivalent of about eight tubs of ice cream!

The stomach has five sections, and each one plays an important part...

The **Corpus** is the largest part of the stomach. Its role is to contract rhythmically to mix eaten food and stomach acid.

The **Antrum** holds partially digested food before sending it to the small intestine.

The **Fundus** collects gases formed during digestion.

The **Pylorus** contains the pyloric sphincter, which controls when the stomach empties its contents into the small intestine.

The **Cardia** prevents food from going back up the esophagus (windpipe).

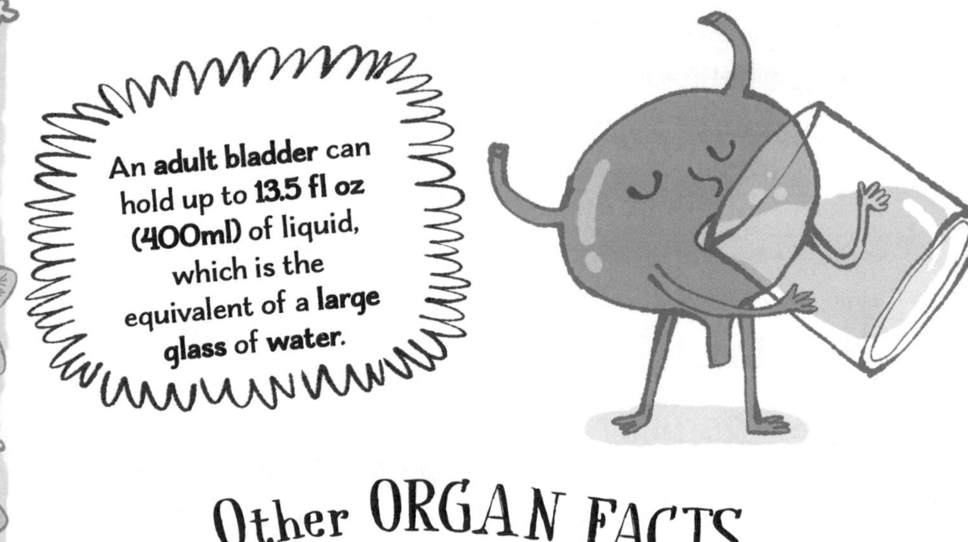

Other ORGAN FACTS

The **biggest** organ in the human body is our **skin**!

The **appendix**, unlike most other organs, **doesn't have a function** in the human body.

Some **organs** are called **hollow organs**. This means that they are **empty** in the **middle**. These include the **stomach**, **intestine**, and **bladder**.

Kidneys filter our blood to remove waste. They take the waste products to our **bladder,** where they are **weeded out**. The kidneys also return **vitamins, amino acids, glucose, and hormones** into the body.

The **intestines** get all the necessary **nutrients** from the **food we eat**, which they provide to the **rest of our body**.

The liver can regenerate. This means it can partially repair itself.

The small intestine is up to 22 feet (7 meters) long. When stretched out, that's taller than a giraffe!

Piles of POO FACTS

Though **POO** contains indigestible **food**, trillions of **bacteria, mucus,** and **dead cells,** it is around **70 percent water.**

Bat poo, also known as "**guano,**" has been used by soldiers to make **explosives**.

Sloths do a weekly **poo dance**. They hold onto tree trunks with their front legs, stand on their hind legs, and **shake their bodies** from side to side as they relieve themselves!

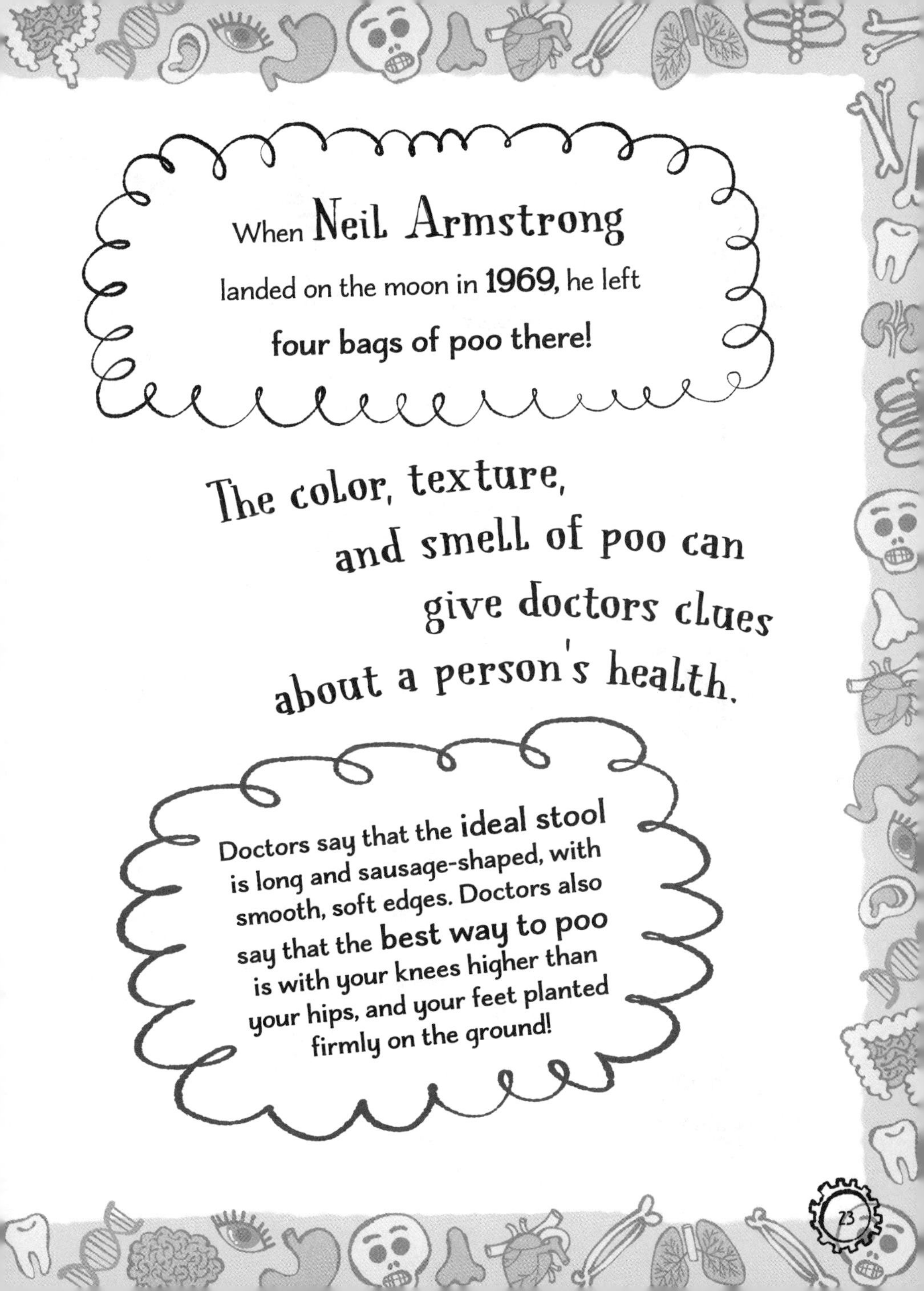

When **Neil Armstrong** landed on the moon in **1969**, he left **four bags of poo there!**

The color, texture, and smell of poo can give doctors clues about a person's health.

Doctors say that the **ideal stool** is long and sausage-shaped, with smooth, soft edges. Doctors also say that the **best way to poo** is with your knees higher than your hips, and your feet planted firmly on the ground!

General FACTS

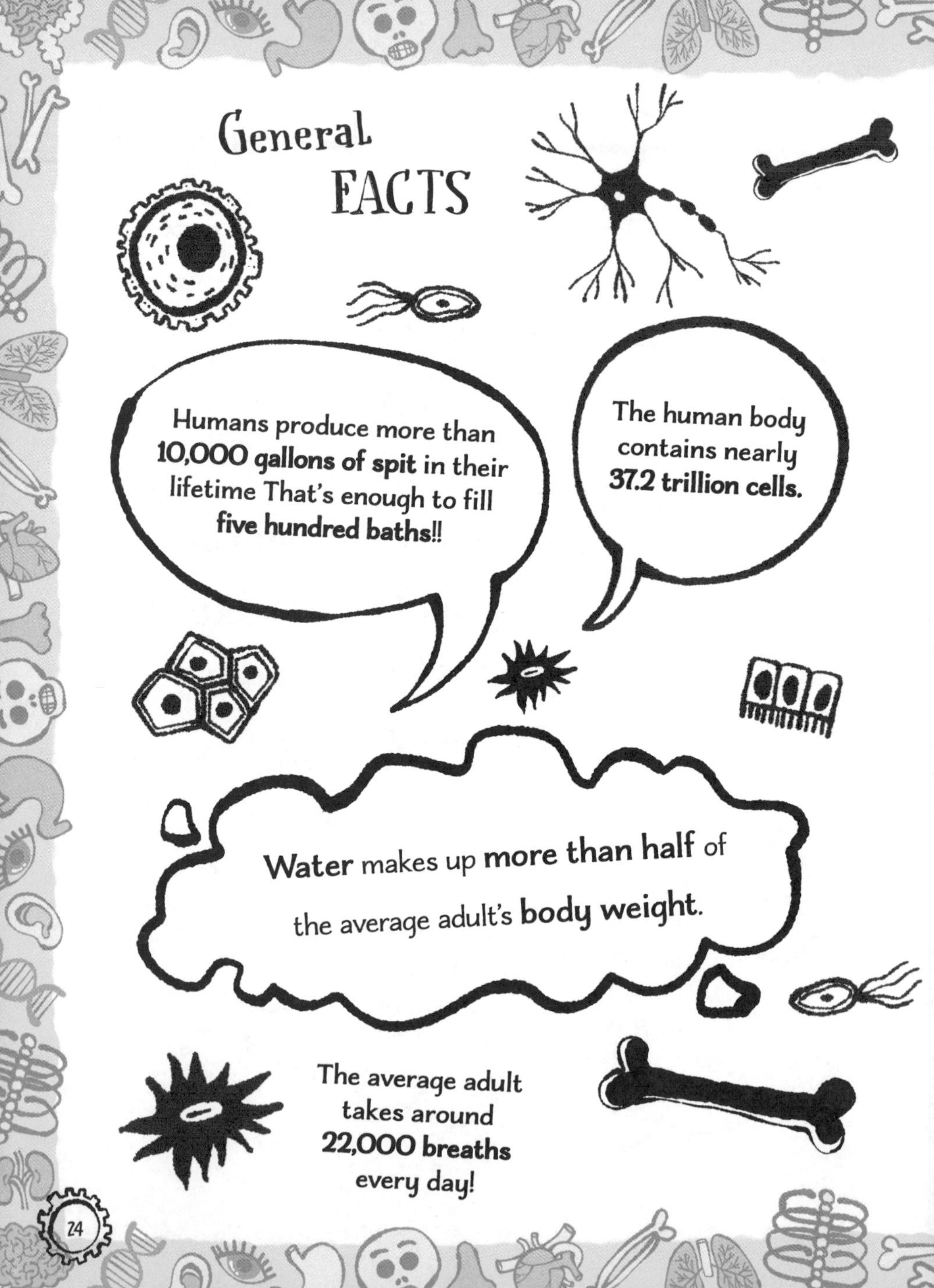

The **world's oldest** recorded person lived to **122** years and **164** days. **Jeanne Louise Calment**, from France, lived between **1875** and **1997**. Remarkably, Jeanne was still bicycling up until she was **100!**

Throughout their lifetime, most people will spend an average of **one whole year sitting on the toilet**!

The human nose can detect up to a trillion different smells.

Our **big toes** can bear **40 percent** of our **body weight.**

SPORTS

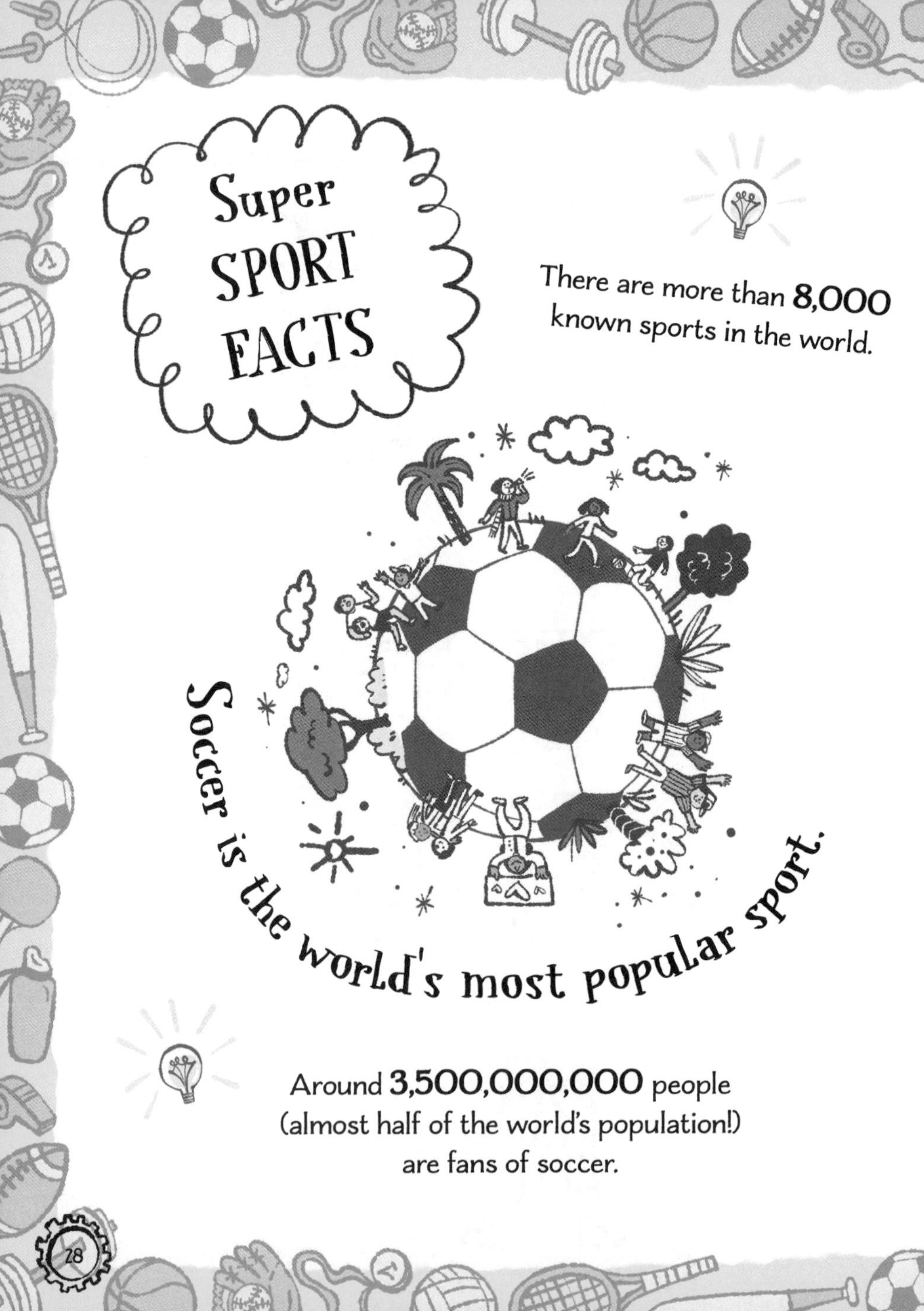

Super SPORT FACTS

There are more than **8,000** known sports in the world.

Soccer is the world's most popular sport.

Around **3,500,000,000** people (almost half of the world's population!) are fans of soccer.

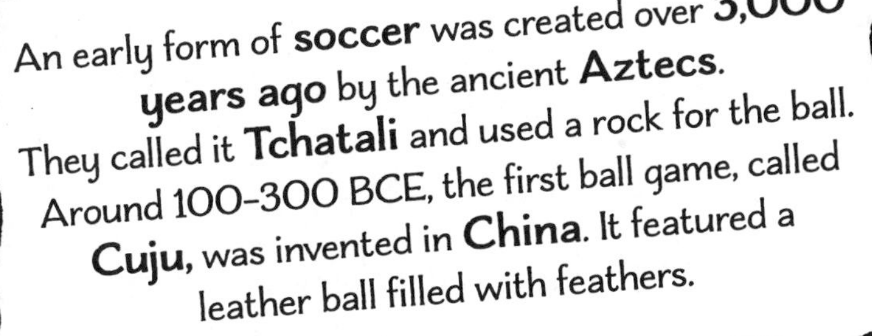

An early form of **soccer** was created over **3,000 years ago** by the ancient **Aztecs.** They called it **Tchatali** and used a rock for the ball. Around 100–300 BCE, the first ball game, called **Cuju,** was invented in **China**. It featured a leather ball filled with feathers.

The **fastest projectile speed** in any **moving ball game** is around **188 mph (302 kph)**. This is in a game called **Jai alai** (also known as pelota).

BASE jumping is the world's most **dangerous sport**. "BASE" stands for the four categories of objects from which people jump off with parachutes: **buildings**, **antennae** (radio masts), **spans** (bridges), and **earth** (cliffs).

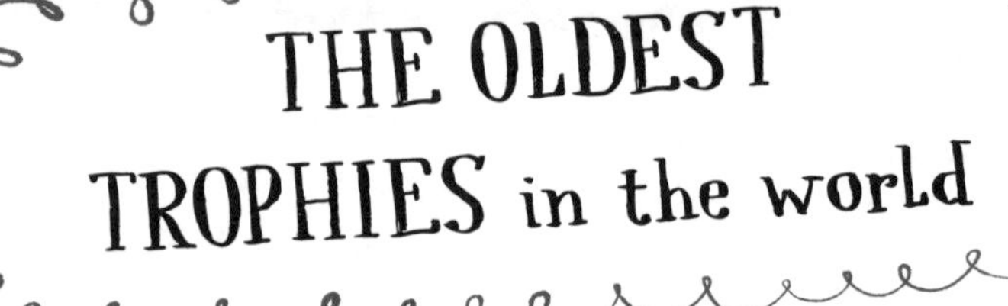

10. **Stanley Cup** (Ice Hockey)
First awarded in 1893. Made in **Canada**.

9. **Ashes Urn** (Cricket)
First awarded in 1883. Made in **Australia**.

8. **Calcutta Cup** (Rugby)
First awarded in 1879. Made in **India**.

7. **Wimbledon Trophies** (Tennis)
Men's Singles in 1887 and Women's Singles in 1886.
Made in **England**.

6. **Scottish Cup Trophy** (Soccer)
First awarded in 1874. Made in **Scotland**.

5. **Claret Jug** (Golf)
First awarded in 1873. Made in **Scotland**.

4. **America's Cup** (Sailing)
First awarded in 1851. Made in **England**.

3. **Royal Musselburgh Old Club Cup** (Golf)

First awarded in 1774. Made in **Scotland.**

2. **Scorton Silver Arrow** (Archery)

First awarded in 1673. Made in **England.**

1. **Carlisle Bells** (Horse Racing)

First awarded in 1599. Made in **England.**

THE OLDEST SPORTS in the world

3. Wrestling

Although its official competitive debut happened in the 1830s, evidence has been found that it was first done **15,300** years ago.

2. Running

Evidence has been found of the earliest of racing competitions alse taking place **15,300** years ago. It officially became a sport in **1831**.

1. Javelin

An ancient hunting javelin has been found that dates back **280,000 years!** It became an official sport at the **Ancient Olympics** in **708 BCE.**

Most watched SPORTS EVENTS

1. **Tour de France**–3.5 billion. The most famous cycling race in the world. Millions of people line the roads to watch, and billions watch on TV around the world.
2. **Men's Football World Cup**–3.3 billion. Held every four years, the best football nations in the world compete.
3. **Cricket World Cup**–2.6 billion.
4. **Summer Olympics**–2 billion.
5. **Winter Olympics**–2 billion.
6. **Women's Football World Cup**–1.1 billion.
7. **UEFA Champions League**–380 million.
8. **Super Bowl**–110 million.

Most watched SPORTS according to Global Fanbase

1. Soccer–3.5 billion.
2. Cricket–2.5 billion.
3. Basketball–2.4 billion.
4. Hockey–2.2 billion.
5. Tennis–1 billion.
6. Volleyball–900 million.
7. Table tennis–850 million.
8. Baseball–500 million.
9. American football–410 million.
10. Rugby–400 million.

THE OLYMPICS

In ancient Greece, athletes competed **naked**!

The **first Olympic Games** took place in the **8th century BCE**, in **Olympia, Greece**. They were held every four years for 12 centuries. Then, in the **4th century CE**, all pagan festivals were banned by **Emperor Theodosius**. The Olympics were resurrected about 1,500 years later, and the first **Modern Olympics** were held in **1896** in **Greece**.

Each ancient Olympics lasted for five or six **months**!

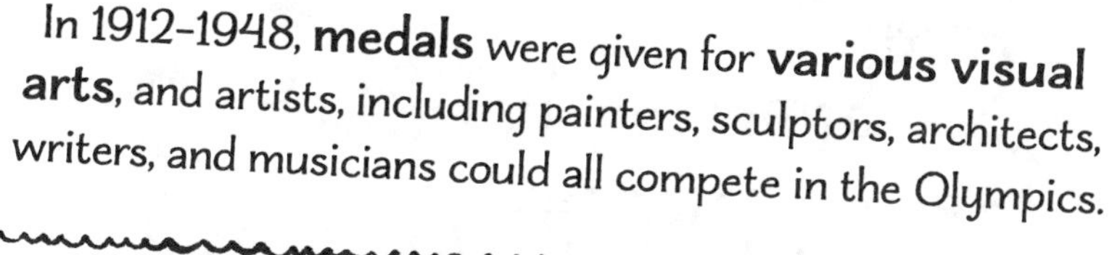

There are some sports that used to be in the Olympic Games but **are no longer included**. These include solo synchronized swimming, tug of war, rope climbing, hot air ballooning, dueling pistol, tandem bicycle, and an obstacle swimming race.

The **five rings motif**, which was designed in 1913, represents the **five inhabited continents** of the world.

The six **olympic colors**—blue, yellow, black, green, red, and the white background—were chosen because every nation's **flag** contains at least one of them.

Sporting WORLD RECORDS

The world's **fastest** person is **Usain Bolt** from **Jamaica**. He ran **100 m** in **9.58 seconds**, and holds the **200 m world record** too.

Ryohei Masuda set the record for **fastest MMA knockout** of all time in **2008**, when he knocked out his opponent in a mere **two seconds!**

Laura Dekker, from the **Netherlands**, became the **youngest person to circumnavigate the globe** (sail around the whole world) solo, at the **age of 16**, from 2010 to 2011.

François-Marie Dibon, from **France**, holds the **world record** for completing the **most bungee jumps** in a 24-hour period, with a whopping **765 jumps**.

Kenyan runner, **Eliud Kipchoge,** holds the world record for the **fastest marathon** time, completing the **26.2-mile race** (42.2 km) in **2 hours, 1 minute,** and **9 seconds**, in **Berlin,** in September 2022.

The **longest tennis match** in history happened in 2010, when **John Isner** from the **US**, and **Nicolas Mahut** from **France** went head-to-head at **Wimbledon**, and played for an astonishing **11 hours and 5 minutes.**

The world's **strongest** person is arguably **Zydrunas Savickas** from **Lithuania.** He has won 'Lithuania's Strongest Man" 17 times, "Europe's Strongest Man" 3 times, and "World's Strongest Man" 4 times.

Kenichi Horie, from **Japan**, was the first person to **sail solo nonstop** across the **Pacific** in **1962**, and also became the **oldest person** to do so in **2022**, at the age of **83**.

Weird and Wonderful SPORTS FACTS

In **tennis**, if a player's **hat falls off**, it counts as an **unintentional hindrance**, and opponents will replay the point.

The London Olympics of 2012 were the first ever Olympic Games that had **female athletes** from **all participating countries**.

In **2002**, a **long-distance runner** from the **US**, **Tom Johnson**, raced against a **horse** for **50 miles** (**80.5 km**). He ran the distance in **five hours 45 minutes**, beating the horse by **ten seconds**!

Soccer player **Joe Sheerin** was called up for the English team, **Chelsea,** in the **last 60 seconds** of their match against **Wimbledon** in **1997**. He never played another game for them and holds the **record** for the **shortest Premier League career.**

Japan is home to the **world's largest bowling alley,** which has **116 lanes.**

Baseball player Ray Caldwell pitched a complete game after he was **struck by lightning** in the middle of the match. His team, the **Cleveland Indians**, still won!

Most UNUSUAL SPORTS

Competitive sheep shearing

This sport has an annual event in **New Zealand** called the **Golden Shears International Championships**, to find out which competitor is the world's fastest sheep shearer. This sport has now spread to Australia, the US, and parts of Europe.

Lawnmower racing

This funny sport sees competitors **riding modified lawnmowers**. The engines remain, but the blades are removed for safety. Originally conceived in a pub in the **UK** in **1973**, there is now a British Lawn Mower Racing Association, and the sport has spread in both location and popularity.

Wife carrying

According to legend, this **Finnish** sport is a modern version of the **ancient custom of wife stealing**. Thankfully, wives are no longer stolen in this comical sport and only consenting partners take part in the race!

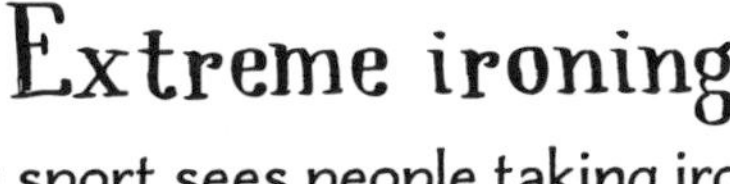

Extreme ironing

This sport sees people taking ironing boards to remote locations and **ironing while competing in thrilling activities**. Invented in the **UK** in **1997**, a knitwear factory employee came home from work with chores to do, but really wanted to go rock climbing. So, he decided to combine his ironing chore with his activity! The Extreme Ironing Bureau say that this hilarious sport "combines the thrills of an **extreme outdoor activity** with the satisfaction of a **well-pressed shirt**."

HISTORY

Historical RECORDS

The **oldest tribe** in the world are the **San People**, who have been living in **Southern Africa** for at least **30,000** years. The San have the most diverse and distinct **DNA** of all **indigenous African groups**.

The **oldest cave painting** can be found in the **Cueva del Castillo**, or **Cave of the Castle**, in **Spain**. It dates back more than **40,000** years.

The **biggest war** in history was **World War II**. This was the **deadliest** and most **destructive** war, with an estimated **50** to **85 million casualties** over its **six-year period**.

Iran is the **oldest** country in the **world.** It was founded in **3200 BCE.**

The **oldest food** in the world that humans made themselves is believed to be **bread**, which dates back over **30,000** years.

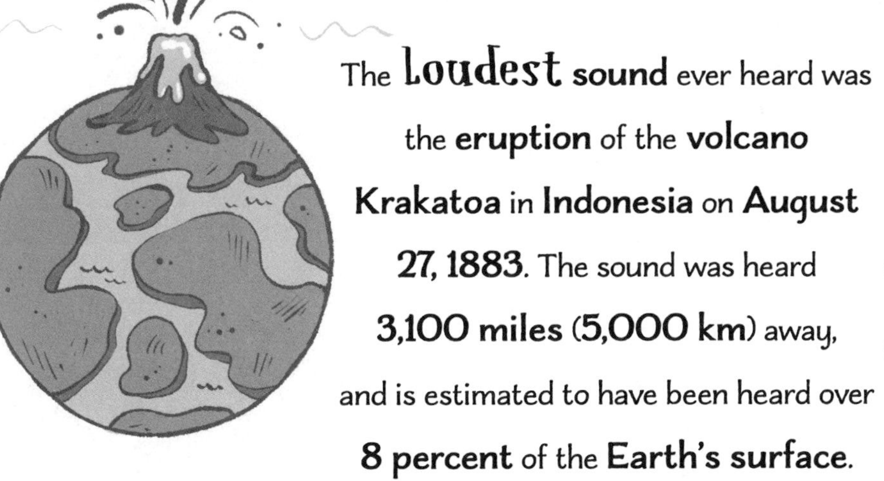

The **Loudest sound** ever heard was the **eruption** of the **volcano Krakatoa** in **Indonesia** on **August 27, 1883**. The sound was heard **3,100 miles (5,000 km)** away, and is estimated to have been heard over **8 percent** of the **Earth's surface.**

The **newest** internationally recognized country in the world is **South Sudan**, in **Africa**, which gained **independence** in **2011.**

EARLY Humans

Cave paintings by early humans have helped **scientists** find out about **early animals**, such as **mammoths**.

The first humans lived over 300,000 years ago.

The **hand ax** is believed to be the **earliest tool** that humans made in **prehistoric times**, and it was used for more than a **million years**. It was useful for cutting **meat** and **wood**, and helped early humans evolve, because by cutting and cooking their meat their **brains developed**.

Our **closest relatives** are **chimpanzees** and **bonobos**, and we share a whopping **98.7 percent** of our **DNA** with them.

Around **8 billion** people live on **Earth** today, and about **117 billion** people have ever lived on Earth.

The first humans lived in Africa and over time, traveled across the world.

ANCIENT EGYPT

The **ancient Egyptians preserved** the **bodies** of important people through **mummification**. They built **special tombs** to be buried in, which they filled with their favorite things. Some pharaohs built their tombs in the shape of **giant pyramids**.

Egyptian people were ruled by **kings** and **queens** called **pharaohs**.

The ancient Egyptians were **experts** at **farming** and **construction**. They grew crops, such as **wheat**, **barley**, **fruit**, and **vegetables**. They also grew **flax** to make clothes, and **papyrus** to make paper.

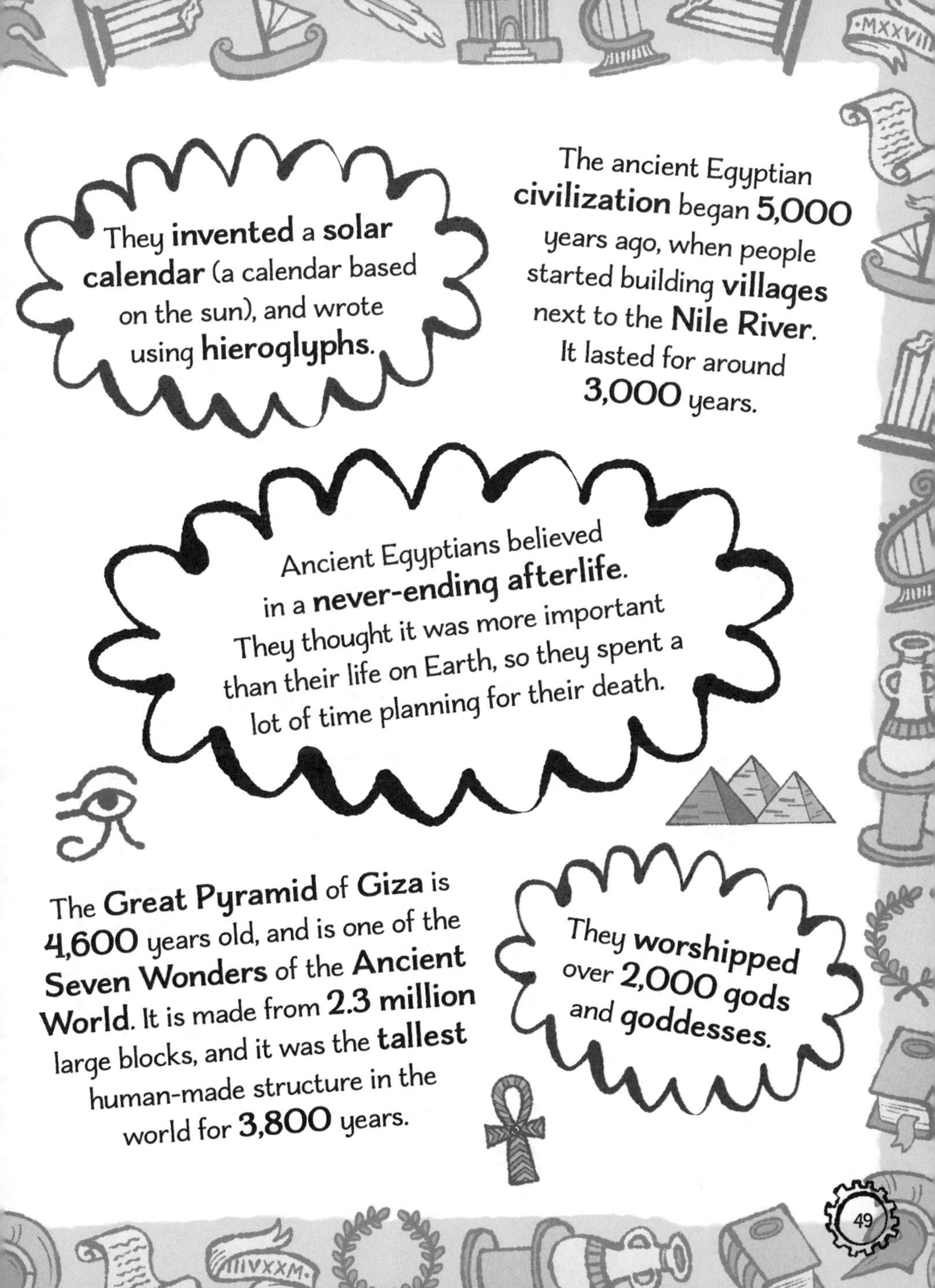

They **invented** a **solar calendar** (a calendar based on the sun), and wrote using **hieroglyphs**.

The ancient Egyptian **civilization** began **5,000** years ago, when people started building **villages** next to the **Nile River**. It lasted for around **3,000** years.

Ancient Egyptians believed in a **never-ending afterlife**. They thought it was more important than their life on Earth, so they spent a lot of time planning for their death.

The **Great Pyramid** of **Giza** is **4,600** years old, and is one of the **Seven Wonders** of the **Ancient World**. It is made from **2.3 million** large blocks, and it was the **tallest** human-made structure in the world for **3,800** years.

They **worshipped** over **2,000 gods** and **goddesses**.

ANCIENT GREECE

About **2,500** years ago, Greece was one of the most **important** places in the ancient world.

Greece was divided up into **city states**, such as **Athens**, **Sparta**, **Corinth**, and **Olympia**. They often fought each other, but they also joined together to **fight** bigger enemies, like the **Persian Empire**.

Greek **gods** and **goddesses** were seen to be very much like humans, but they lived **forever** and were much more **powerful**. From time to time, gods would interfere in what was going on.

It is thought that the Greeks invented the **yo-yo**, as an early yo-yo toy found by scientists dated back to **500 BCE**.

The **marathon** came from ancient Greece. It is believed that a man called **Pheidippides** ran **26 miles (42 km)** from the **city** of **Marathon** to the capital city, **Athens** in order to announce the Greeks' defeat over the **Persians**.

The Greeks believed that **gods** and **goddesses** watched over them, living high above **Mount Olympus,** in a palace in the clouds. From here, they kept an eye on life below.

The Greeks were great **thinkers, warriors, writers, actors, athletes, artists, architects,** and **politicians.**

In the **300s BCE, Alexander the Great** ruled Greece. Alexander led his army to **conquer** a huge **empire** that was much **larger** than the modern country of Greece we know today.

ANCIENT ROME

Rome was founded in **753 BCE** by its first king, **Romulus**.

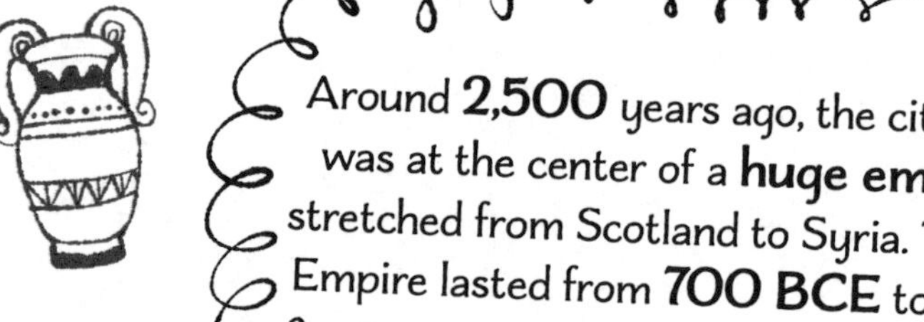

Around **2,500** years ago, the city of Rome was at the center of a **huge empire** that stretched from Scotland to Syria. The Roman Empire lasted from **700 BCE** to **476 AD**.

Like the Greeks, the Romans had lots of different **gods** and **goddesses**.

They also **borrowed** new gods from the people they conquered, like the **goddess Isis** from Egypt, and **Mithras** from Iran. Some emperors were declared gods too, usually after they died. The ancient Romans hoped this would make emperors even more powerful and respected.

At the peak of its **power**, Rome ruled more than **45 million** people across **Europe, North Africa**, and **Asia**. Its army was the most powerful in the world.

In **49 BCE**, Rome's greatest general was **Julius Caesar**. He had complete control of the army, but he wanted to rule Rome the way that past kings did. Some senators didn't like this and they **killed** him in **44 BCE**. But by this point it was too late—Julius Caesar had changed Rome forever.

A few years later, **Julius Caesar's** adopted son **Octavius** took power and became the first Emperor of Rome.

Enslaved people were **bought** and **sold** all around the empire. You could buy or win your freedom.

FAMOUS PEOPLE Throughout History

Here are ten of the most influential figures in human history, with a fact about each that you may never have heard before.

Muhammad

The founder of Islam is such an important figure in the Muslim religion that his name is now one of the most popular names in the world.

William Shakespeare

From 1585-1593, the playwright disappeared from records, and this period remains a mystery. Historians call it his "lost years."

Marie Curie

Curie conducted pioneering work on the treatment of cancer using radioactivity. She was the first woman to win a Nobel Prize, and the first person to win two.

Aristotle

Alongside his important work in math, psychology, and logic, the ancient Greek philosopher is also credited as one of the founders of zoology.

Rosa Parks

The American activist who is known as "the mother of freedom," for her refusal to accept racial injustice, also has a species of spider named after her! It's called Aptostichus rosaparksae.

Napoleon

This French leader is said to have disguised himself in common clothing and asked people on the streets what they "thought of Napoleon"—without telling them who he was!

Martin Luther King, Jr.

This Civil Rights leader dedicated his life to the nonviolent struggle for racial equality in the US. Because of his high intelligence, he started college at just 15.

Charles Darwin

Known as the father of evolution, when Darwin was a student, he formed a club for the purpose of dining on exotic "birds and beasts, which were before unknown to human palate."

Emmeline Pankhurst

The British activist and founder of the Suffragettes could apparently read from the age of 3 and read long novels by 9. This may explain why she was a natural-born leader.

Leonardo da Vinci

The forward-thinking artist and scientist never went to school, and was mostly self-educated. Not bad for a genius painter, engineer, sculptor, and architect!

On **pirate ships** in the **Georgian era** (**1714-1832**), **carpenters** would carry out **amputations** if necessary, because there were **rarely any doctors**!

Author **Morgan Robertson** predicted the **sinking** of the **Titanic** in **1898**. He published his novella, **The Wreck of the Titan**, which featured a huge British **ocean liner** with limited lifeboats, which hit an **iceberg** and sunk in the same ocean as the Titanic.

Ancient Romans gargled **human urine** to freshen their breaths, like a kind of **mouthwash**!

Before the **invention** of **toilet paper**, **Americans** would use **corn cobs**.

An **ancient Greek boxer** was so jealous of his rival, **Theagenes of Thasos**, that he decided to **attack a statue of him**. However, he hit the statue a little too hard and it fell over, **crushing him to death!**

In the **Middle Ages**, more than **75 million Europeans** were killed by **rats**! They died of the **Black Death**, which was spread by **rats**.

The **Inca** people of **Peru** made **jewelry** out of the **toenail clippings** of **llamas!**

Ancient Egyptians thought they could **cure baldness** in a bizarre way. They rubbed **fat** from animals on their **heads**. They also thought they could cure **gray hair** with an **ointment** made from rotten **donkey liver.**

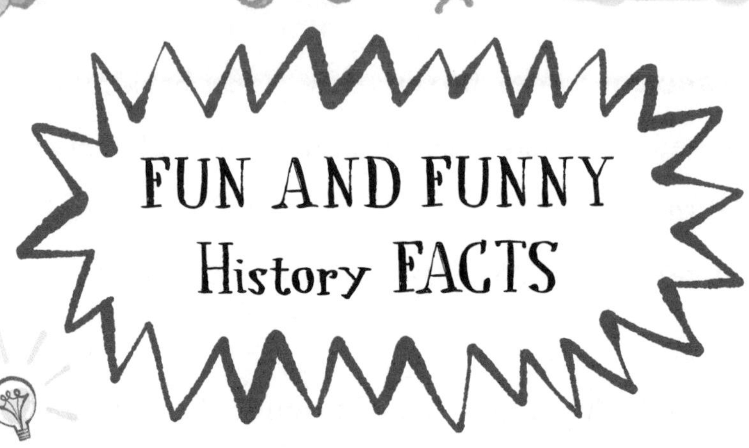

In **Ancient Rome, Emperor Gaius** made one of his **favorite horses** a **senator** when he came to power.

The **Last Letter** to be added to the **alphabet** was actually **"J"** not **"Z"**.

An **Egyptian Pharaoh**, kept **flies** away in an imaginative and cruel way–by **smearing honey** on his **slaves** so that the flies went to them instead.

In the **1840s**, when having their **pictures taken,** people would say **"Prunes!"** instead of **"Cheese!"** This was to keep their **mouths stiff**, as big smiles in photographs were seen as **childish**.

Paris's **Eiffel Tower** was originally meant for **Barcelona**. When its designer, **Gustav Eiffel**, presented his design, they thought it was **too ugly**. He then pitched it as a temporary landmark for the **World Fair in Paris in 1889**, and it's been there ever since.

Ketchup was once sold as a **medicine**. In the **1830s**, it was believed that the sauce could **cure** almost anything.

In **1905**, an **11-year-old boy** left a **cup of water** and **bicarbonate of soda** outside overnight, with a wooden stirrer in. The next day he discovered the mixture had **frozen**, and **ice lollipops** were born! They were originally called **Epsicles** because the boy's name was **Frank Epperson.**

Though rare, there were **female gladiators** in **Ancient Rome**. They were called **Gladiatrix** or **Gladiatrices.**

FOOD and DRINK

Phenomenal FOOD FACTS

There are more than 2,000 different fruits.

There are more than 20,000 different vegetables.

Three billion cups of tea are consumed every day.

Two billion cups of coffee are consumed every day.

Food menus first popped up in Europe in the **mid-1700s** to accommodate high-class residents during dinner parties.

Candy floss was bizarrely invented by a dentist!

Cashew nuts don't grow like other nuts, they grow on cashew apples!

In **1961**, Yuri Gagarin became the first person to travel into space, as well as the first person to **eat in space!** His meal was beef and liver paste squeezed from a tube, followed by a tube of chocolate sauce.

SWEET and SOUR

Here is a list of the **sweetest fruits in the world** (per grams of sugar in a serving cup).

1. Raisins-108g
2. Zante currants-90g
3. Dried peaches-67g
4. Lychees-29g
5. Pomegranates-24g
6. Mangoes-23g
7. Grapes-23g
8. Persimmons-21g
9. Cherries-20g
10. Apples-19g
11. Bananas-18g
12. Pears, watermelons, and oranges-17g

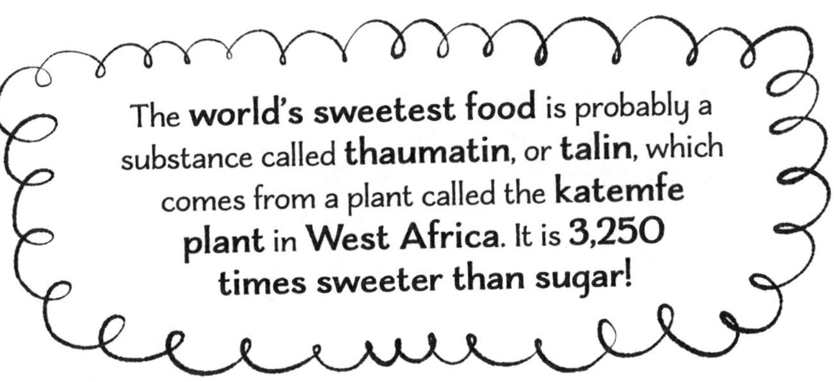

The **world's sweetest food** is probably a substance called **thaumatin**, or **talin**, which comes from a plant called the **katemfe plant** in **West Africa**. It is **3,250 times sweeter than sugar!**

The **world's most sour food** is the **Umeboshi Sour Plum**. This comes from the **Ume fruit**, which is a close cousin of **plums and apricots**.

Umeboshi sour plums are **preserved** through **salting**, which gives this **treat** an extremely **sour** and **intense flavor**.

HOT and COLD

The hottest peppers in the world

These are measured using the **Scoville scale**, which is a measurement of how **spicy** foods are.

1. Pepper X
2. Apollo Pepper
3. Dragon's Breath Pepper
4. Carolina Reaper
5. Komodo Dragon Pepper

Coldest foods in the world

The coldest foods in the world are made with **liquid nitrogen**, which can reach temperatures as low as **minus 320° F (minus 196° C)**. **Ice cream** and other frozen foods use this method to keep them cold.

Flash freezing

The founder of **Birds Eye Frozen Foods**, Clarence Birdseye, introduced flash freezing to the world in **1924**. This meant that **fresh food** could be **frozen** and **defrosted** in a matter of hours, keeping it fresher for longer, and **safer** for consumption.

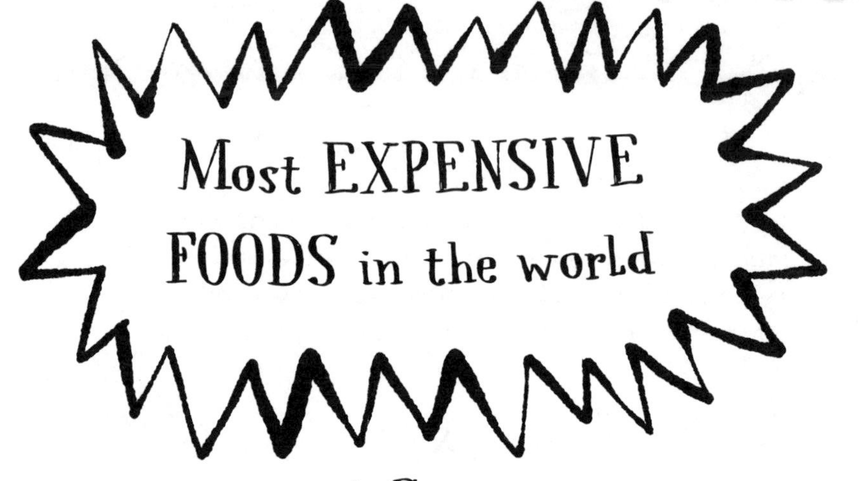

Most EXPENSIVE FOODS in the world

1. Saffron

This **spice** is nicknamed **"red gold,"** and is used as a **coloring agent** in food. Weight for weight, it is **more expensive than gold**. It takes as many as **300,000 flowers**, to produce **2.2 lb (1 kg)** of saffron.

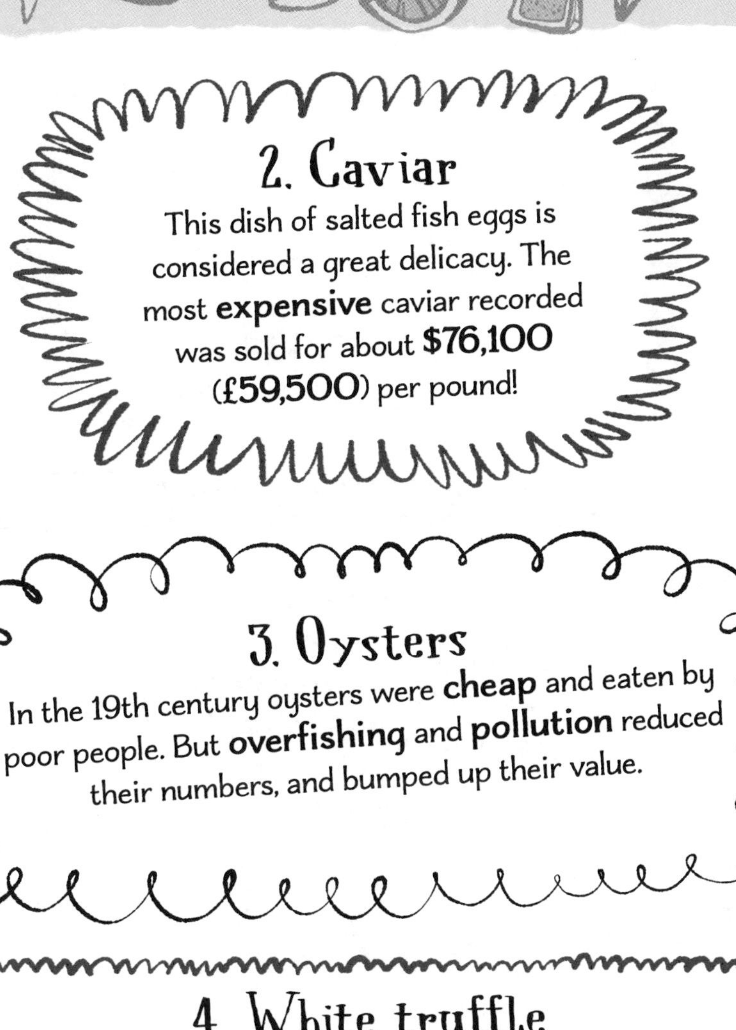

2. Caviar

This dish of salted fish eggs is considered a great delicacy. The most **expensive** caviar recorded was sold for about **$76,100 (£59,500)** per pound!

3. Oysters

In the 19th century oysters were **cheap** and eaten by poor people. But **overfishing** and **pollution** reduced their numbers, and bumped up their value.

4. White truffle

This is the **rarest** type of truffle. It is found in Northern Italy, where trained **dogs** are used to help sniff them out. The most expensive white truffle on record sold for **$211,000 (£165,000)**.

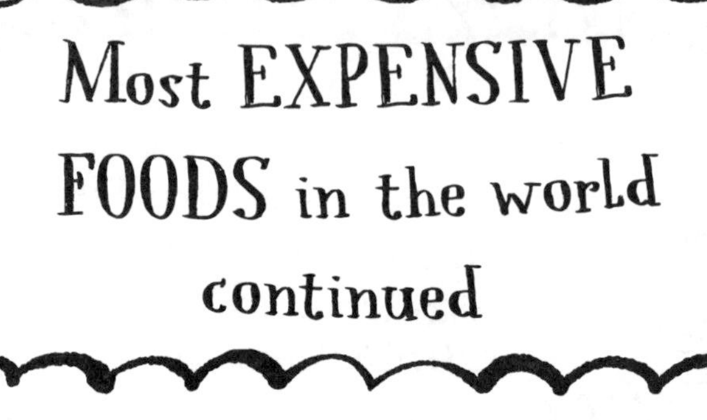

Most EXPENSIVE FOODS in the world continued

5. Iberico ham

Produced in Spain and Portugal, the finest Iberico ham comes from **free range pigs** that eat only **acorns** in the last period of their life. The most **expensive** Iberico ham sold for more than **$3,835** (£3,000).

6. Wagyu beef

This **Japanese** beef is described as **melting in the mouth**.

It can cost up to **$1,400** (£1,100) per pound in Japan.

7. Kopi luwak coffee

Selling for up to **$1,500 (£1,100)** per pound, Kopi luwak, or civet coffee, is made from coffee beans that have been **eaten**, partly digested and then **pooed** by **Asian palm civet cats**. Though it might not sound very appetizing, this is said to be the **smoothest coffee in the world**.

8. Foie gras

Foie gras is a **pâté** made from **duck** or **goose liver** that has been fattened (up to ten times its normal size). This practice dates back to as early as 2500 BCE, when the **ancient Egyptians** learned that many birds could be **fattened** through forced overfeeding.

- **Berries** including strawberries, raspberries, blueberries, acai berries, goji berries, cranberries, and grapes.
- **Fish** including salmon, tuna, mackerel, herring, trout, anchovies, and sardines.
- **Leafy greens** including spinach, swiss chard, kale, collard greens, and mustard greens.
- **Nuts** including hazelnuts, walnuts, almonds, and pecans.

Olive oil

Whole grains

including oats, brown rice, buckwheat, fonio (an ancient grain), and quinoa.

Yogurt

Cruciferous vegetables

including broccoli, brussels sprouts, cabbage, cauliflower, radishes, and turnips.

Legumes

including kidney, black, red, and garbanzo beans, as well as soybeans and peas.

Tomatoes

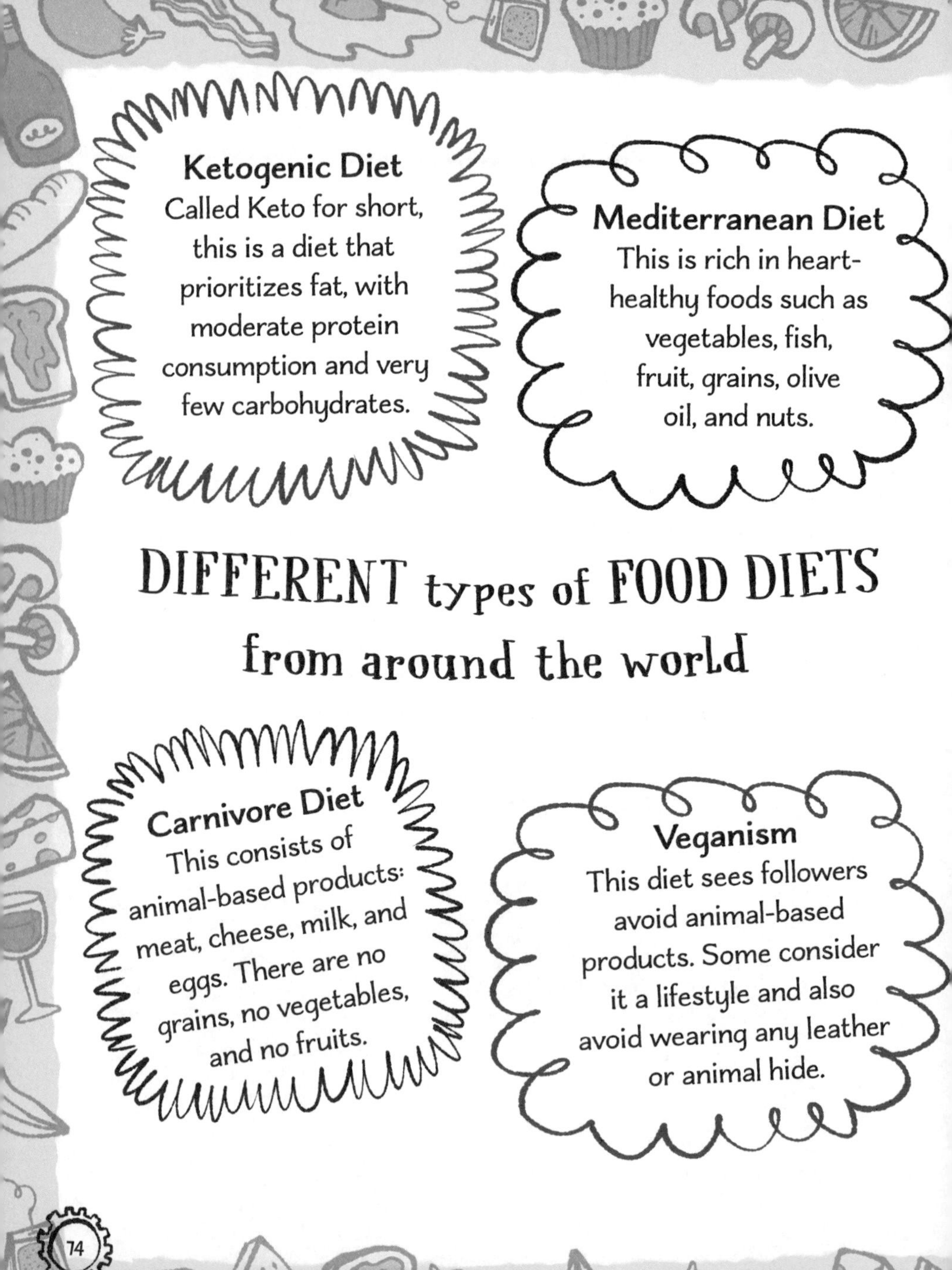

Ketogenic Diet

Called Keto for short, this is a diet that prioritizes fat, with moderate protein consumption and very few carbohydrates.

Mediterranean Diet

This is rich in heart-healthy foods such as vegetables, fish, fruit, grains, olive oil, and nuts.

DIFFERENT types of FOOD DIETS from around the world

Carnivore Diet

This consists of animal-based products: meat, cheese, milk, and eggs. There are no grains, no vegetables, and no fruits.

Veganism

This diet sees followers avoid animal-based products. Some consider it a lifestyle and also avoid wearing any leather or animal hide.

The Paleo or "Caveman" Diet

could be considered a **cousin** of the **carnivore** diet. In **addition** to **meat**, followers also eat **fish**, **fruit**, **nuts**, and **seeds**. They avoid **grains**, **dairy**, **processed foods**, **beans**, **legumes**, and **sugars**.

PLACES

RUSSIA
The biggest country in the world

The Russian **culture** views **smiling** as a sign of **weakness.**

Russia's **biggest lake**, **Lake Baikal**, has **more water** than any other lake on Earth, and holds almost a quarter of the fresh water in the world.

Russia is home to **one-fifth of Earth's trees**—an enormous **640 billion!**

Russia is home to the **world's coldest village, Oymyakon**. Winters in this village average **-58°F (-50°C)**. The coldest recorded temperature in Oymyakon is **-96°F (-71°C)**.

Russia has **12 active volcanoes.**

Russia is home to the **world's longest railroad**, the **Trans-Siberian Railway**.

CHINA
The most populated country in the world

If all of China's **railroad lines** were put together, it could loop around the **Earth twice!**

Half of the **world's pigs** live in China.

Paper money was invented in China.

In China, more than **30 million** people live in **caves**.

One in every **five people** in the world is Chinese.

China has a **civilization** that spans more than **5,000 years**.

Some of the **bricks** in the **Great Wall** of China are held together by **rice paper**.

The world's **biggest shopping mall** is in China, and is actually **99 percent** empty.

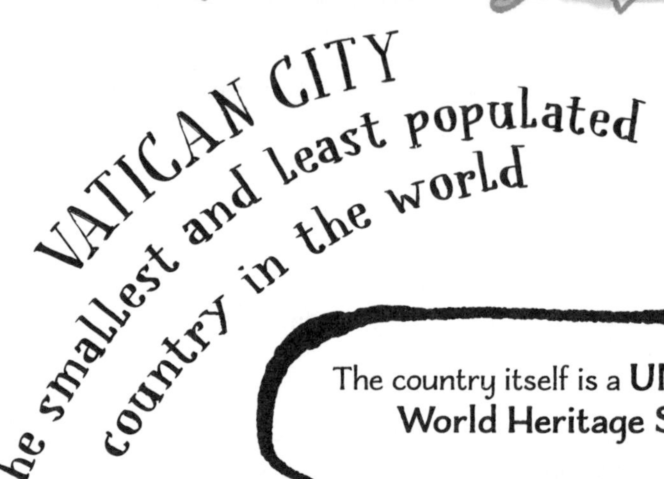

VATICAN CITY

The smallest and least populated country in the world

The country itself is a **UNESCO World Heritage Site.**

The **economy** of the country is largely supported by the sale of postage stamps, tourist mementos, the entry fee for museums, and the sale of publications.

100 percent of Vatican City's **population** is Catholic.

The Vatican City is famous for some of the world's most **popular paintings** and **sculptures**, in cultural sites such as **St. Peter's Basilica**, the **Sistine Chapel**, and the **Vatican museums**.

The Vatican City is ruled by the **Pope**.

TOKYO
The most populated city in the world

Tokyo is home to **38 million people.**

Tokyo has the **highest number** of **Michelin starred restaurants** in the world.

Tokyo has the most **neon signs** in the world.

There is one **vending machine** per 23 citizens.

Tokyo's **busiest intersection, Shibuya Crossing**, is also the world's busiest intersection. An average of **2,500** people cross the intersection **every time the light turns green.**

Other highly populated cities include:

Delhi, India
São Paulo, Brazil
Shanghai, China
Mexico City, Mexico

There are roughly 7,000 LANGUAGES in the world.

The top 10 most spoken languages in the world, and the number of speakers...

1. **Mandarin**–1,377 million
2. **English**–865 million
3. **Spanish**–500 million
4. **Hindi**–430 million
5. **Bengali**–345 million
6. **French**–325 million
7. **Arabic**–315 million
8. **Russian**–265 million
9. **Portuguese**–250 million
10. **Punjabi**–222 million

There are 18 languages that have only one speaker...

From **Brazil**: Apiaká, Diahói, and Kaixána

From **Argentina**: Chaná

From **Venezuela**: Pémono

From **Peru**: Taushiro

From **Colombia**: Tinigua

From **Chile**: Yahgan

From **US**: Patwin, Tolowa, and Wintu-Nomlaki

From **Indonesia**: Dampelas

From **Papua New Guinea**: Lae, Yarawi, and Laua

From **Vanuatu**: Volow

From **Cameroon**: Bikya and Bishuo

CONTINENTS

There are seven continents in the world:

Asia

Africa

North America

South America

Antarctica

Europe

Australia

About **200 million years ago**, all of the continents we know today were one enormous land mass, surrounded by a huge ocean. This **supercontinent** is called **Pangea**, and over the following years it slowly broke apart and **spread out** to form our current continents.

OCEANS

There are five oceans in the world:

Arctic Atlantic Pacific Indian Southern (also known as the Antarctic Ocean)

1. Aurora Borealis

or **Northern Lights**, around the **Arctic**.

A naturally occurring **phenomenon** that happens when solar wind comes into contact with Earth's magnetic field.

2. Mount Everest, Nepal.

This is **world's tallest mountain**, at 29,000 ft (8,849 m) high.

3. Paricutin Volcano, Mexico.

The **volcano surged** suddenly in **1943**. It was then active for nine years, allowing scientists to document its full life cycle.

4. Harbor of Rio de Janeiro,

Brazil. It was discovered by a seafarer in **1502**.

5. Victoria Falls,

Zimbabwe. This is the world's **largest waterfall** based on its width and height combined. Its indigenous name is **Mosi-oa-Tunya**, which means "the smoke that thunders."

6. Grand Canyon,

Arizona, US. It was formed around **five to six million years ago**, when erosion from the **Colorado River** cut a deep channel through layers of rock.

7. Great Barrier Reef,

Queensland, Australia. Visible from space, it's the **world's largest coral reef system**. It is made up of almost 3,000 small reefs and about 900 islands, with thousands of species of marine life.

The other WONDERS of the WORLD

The Seven Modern Wonders of the World

1. **Christ the Redeemer**, Brazil
2. **Petra**, Jordan
3. **Taj Mahal**, India
4. **Great Wall of China**, China
5. **Chichén Itzá**, Mexico
6. **Colosseum**, Italy
7. **Machu Picchu**, Peru

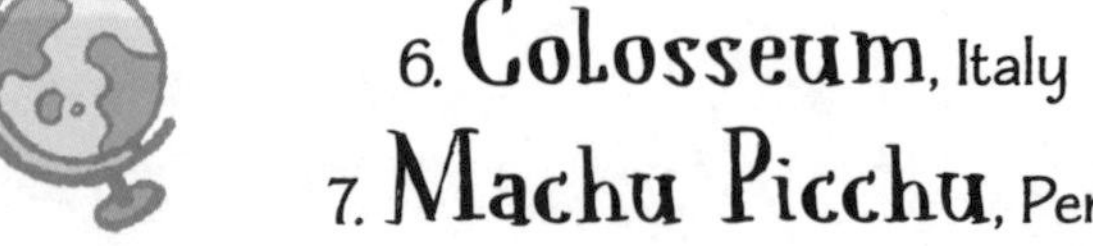

The Seven Wonders of the Ancient World

1. Great Pyramid of Giza, Egypt
2. Colossus of Rhodes, Greece
3. Hanging Gardens of Babylon, Iraq
4. Lighthouse of Alexandria, Egypt
5. Mausoleum at Halicarnassus, Turkey
6. Statue of Zeus at Olympia, Greece
7. Temple of Artemis at Ephesus, Turkey

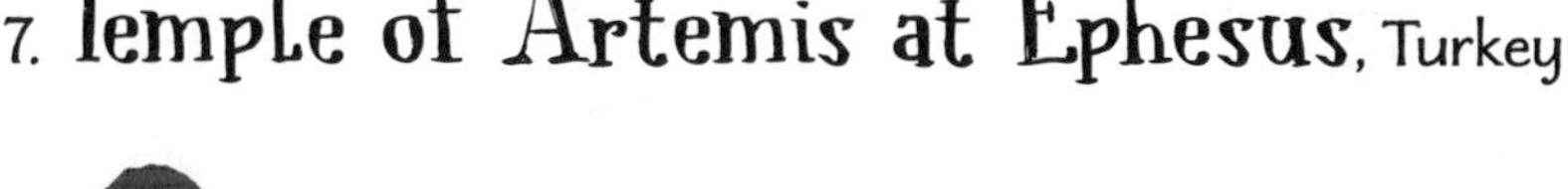

MUSIC

ORCHESTRAS

An **orchestra** is a group that plays instruments together. A large orchestra may consist of around **100** musicians and be called a **"symphony orchestra,"** and a small one might have around **30** players and be known as a **"chamber orchestra."**

Orchestras are usually known for playing classical music and are led by a conductor.

The word "orchestra" is from the semicircular space in front of a stage in a Greek theater.

The instruments in an orchestra fall under four "families"-string, woodwind, brass, and percussion.

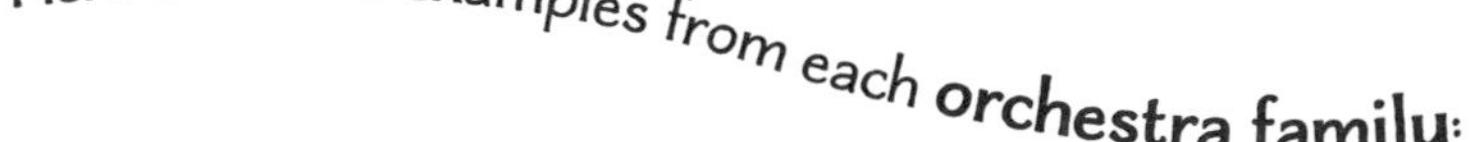

Here are some examples from each **orchestra family**:

STRINGS
violin, double bass, viola, cello, guitar, harp, mandolin.

WOODWIND
flute, clarinet, bassoon, oboe, saxophone, piccolo, tin whistle, recorder, bagpipes, cor anglais.

BRASS
trombone, trumpet, cornet, tuba, tenor horn, french horn, euphonium.

PERCUSSION
piano, tambourine, glockenspiel, triangle, cymbals, chimes, timpani, bass drum, snare drum, celeste.

The instruments are grouped based on their characteristics—such as how musicians play them, their volume, and what kind of sounds they produce.

Interesting INSTRUMENTS

The **LOUDEST** (and largest) instrument in the world is the Boardwalk Hall Auditorium Organ. It lives in New Jersey, US, and its loudest note is six times louder than a steam train's whistle!

The most **expensive** musical instruments in the world are the Stradivarius string instruments made by members of the Italian Stradivari family in the 17th and 18th centuries. They're considered some of the finest instruments ever made.

The most **high-priced** instrument of all time is the MacDonald Stradivarius. This viola is on sale for $45 million (around £37 million). Part of the reason for its high price tag is the fact there are reported to be only ten Stradivarius violas in existence today.

The oldest musical instrument in the world is a **35,000-year-old** flute made of vulture bone.

The **smallest** instrument in the world is the nano harp. It was made in a science lab, and carved in the shape of a guitar. Its strings are one billionth of a foot long, and its sounds are beyond human hearing.

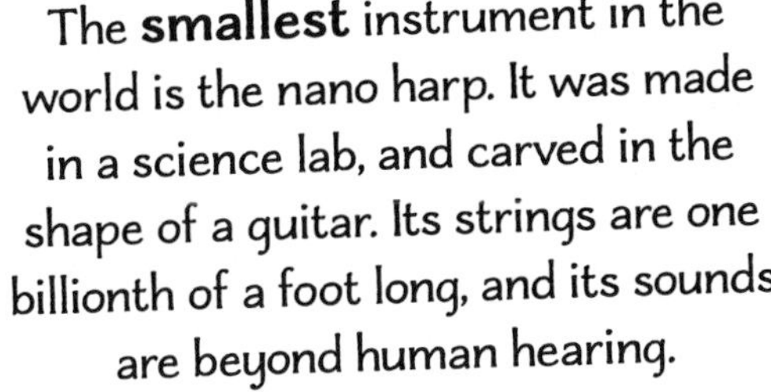

It is said that the **10 most difficult** instruments to learn are: viola, french horn, organ, bagpipes, accordion, oboe, harp, guitar, piano, and cello.

Neil Nayyar is the current world record holder for most instruments played. At age 12, he broke the world record by playing **44** instruments. A year later, he broke his own record by playing **107**. At 17, he could play **117**!

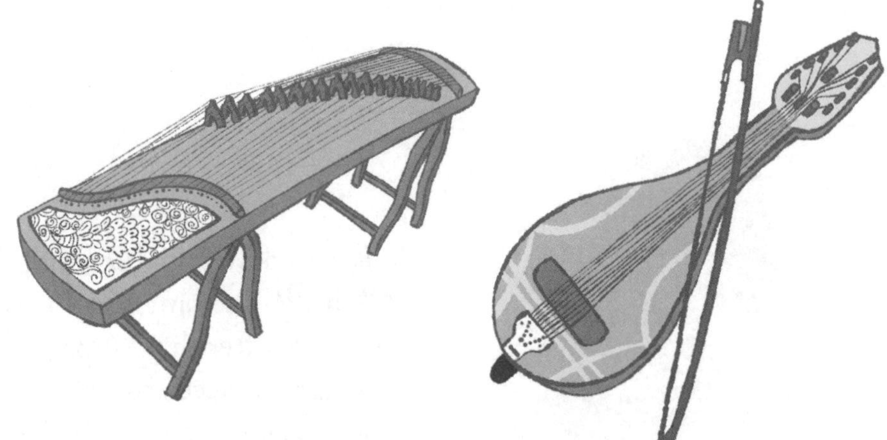

"White Christmas," written by Irving Berlin and recorded by Bing Crosby in 1942, is not only the biggest selling Christmas song but also the **best-selling** single worldwide, with estimated sales of over 50 million copies.

The Beatles are the biggest selling artist on record, with **183 million** records sold. They are often regarded as the most influential band of all time, and although they were active from 1960 to 1970, no more recent artists have managed to top their record.

The first song broadcast on the radio was "O Holy Night" on Christmas Eve in 1906.

The best-selling album on record is Michael Jackson's "Thriller," with an estimated 70 million copies sold worldwide.

In December 1965. **"Jingle Bells"** was broadcast during NASA's Gemini 6A mission, making it the first song played in space!

Magnificent MOZART

Mozart was one of the most enduring and influential composers in history. His body of work includes **21** stage and opera works, **15** masses, more than **50** symphonies, **25** piano concertos, **12** violin concertos, **27** concert arias, **17** piano sonatas, and **26** string quartets.

He was so young when he wrote his first piece for violin and piano (five years old) that he needed his father's help—not to write the music, but to **hold the pencil!**

Mozart composed more than 600 works in his life, and he only lived up to the age of 35.

Mozart spoke an impressive **15** languages.

In 2016, Mozart sold more CDs than Beyoncé. Universal Music Group released a box set commemorating the 225th anniversary of his death, and each box set held **200** CDs!

Mozart kept a range of **animals** throughout his life. He owned a canary, a starling, a dog, and a horse.

He had a **photographic memory** for music.

His father, Leopold Mozart, was a composer too.

Cool CONCERTS

The Beatles helped end racially segregated concerts by refusing to play at segregated events.

In 2006, **Katie Melua** gave a concert at almost 1,000 ft (303 m) below sea level at an oil rig. This earned a world record for "deepest underwater concert."

At a 2010 show in Missouri, US, rock band **Kings of Leon** were forced to leave the stage after playing just three songs. This was because a flock of pigeons were roosting above the stage, and kept **pooing** on the band!

The five **BIGGEST** concerts of all time...

5 The fifth most attended concert, with 1.6 million people, was the **Monsters of Rock Festival** in 1991 (bands included AC/DC and Metallica). It took place in Russia (known as the Soviet Union at the time).

4 Next was French electronic composer and performer, **Jean Michel Jarre** in Paris, France in 1990, where there were 2.5 million attendees.

3 Brazilian musician **Jorge Ben Jor** was next, and he performed in Rio De Janeiro, Brazil, in 1991, to an audience of 3 million.

2 Second on the list was **Jean Michel Jarre** again, and this time he performed in Moscow, Russia in 1997, to an audience of 3.5 million.

1 The biggest concert of all time was **Rod Stewart** in Brazil in 1994 (at the same place as Jorge Ben Jor). He performed to **4.2 million people**! This was a free concert on New Year's Eve, and people came to Copacabana Beach to watch the fireworks and see him perform.

Marvellous MUSIC FACTS

Heartbeats mimic the beat of music. While they don't completely match the rhythm of the music, they **slow down** when listening to slower music and **speed up** when the music is faster.

Studies show that louder music causes a rise in blood pressure, pulse rate, and breathing, and slower music causes them to decrease.

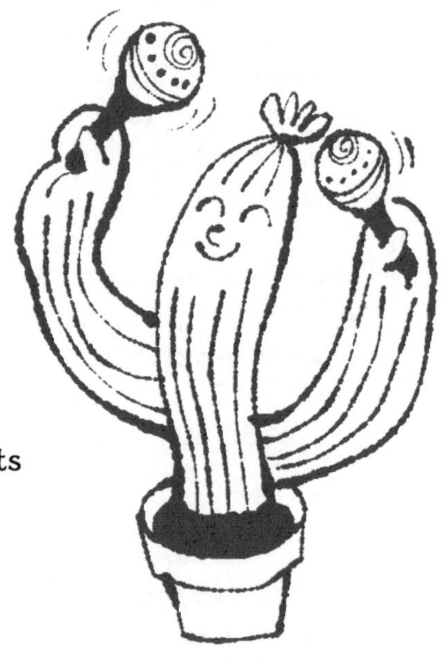

Music helps plants **grow faster.** And according to a study by scientists from South Korea, plants grow at a faster pace when they are played **classical music**.

The musician, **Prince** played a whopping 27 instruments on his debut album, "For You," which was released when he was just **20 years old.**

The world's largest rock band included 953 musicians. In 2016, the Beijing Contemporary Music Academy performed in China with a band that included 349 singers, 154 guitarists, 151 drummers, 100 bassists, 100 keyboard players, and 98 wind instrumentalists!

As of 2022, the global music industry was worth an enormous $26.2 billion (£21.1 billion).

In a 2014 study completed by The Manchester Museum of Science and Industry, "Wannabe" by the British girl group, **The Spice Girls**, was found to be the **catchiest song ever!**

Speaking of catchy songs, a song that gets stuck in your head is called an **"Earworm."**

Music GENRES

Music genres are categories for different styles of music. Songs in each genre will be defined as having some of the same patterns, sounds, or qualities as other songs in the same genre.

Some examples of music genres are...

Pop (which stands for popular), **Rock** (also known as rock & roll), **Hip-hop**, **R'n'B** (which stands for rhythm and blues), **Country**, **Rap**, **Classical**, **Jazz**, **Electronic**, **Indie** (which stands for independent), **Blues**, **Garage**, **Metal**, **Techno**, **Dubstep**, **Drum and bass**, **Grime**, **Punk**, **Folk**, **Alternative**, **Acoustic**, **Soul**, **Funk**, **Traditional**, and **Dance.**

There are also more specific genres, such as K-Pop which stands for Korean pop music, and Britpop which refers to British pop.

Some genres can be mixed together, and these are known as **subgenres**. They include acoustic rock and classic metal.

Many genres also overlap, as songs can be categorized in multiple genres at the same time, and some people don't agree with genre classifications.

There are over 1,200 subgenres of music that have been categorized online. This list continues to grow, as music is always evolving, and the use of electronic instruments means that anything is possible!

Finland has the most metal bands of all countries, with 53.2 heavy metal bands per 100,000 residents.

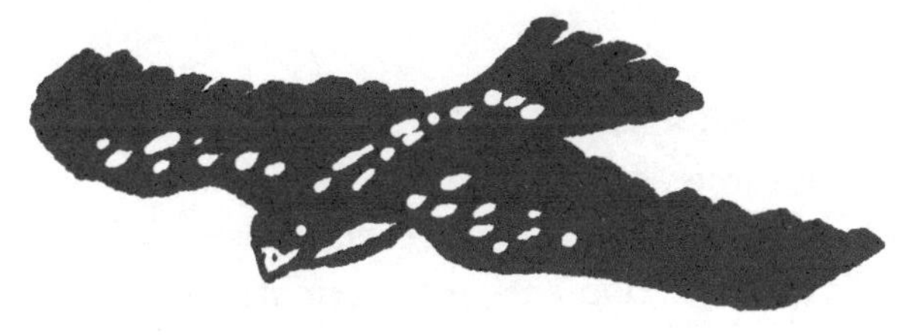

ANIMALS AND NATURE

Ultimate ANIMALS

The biggest animal in the world is the blue whale. It weighs the same as 40 elephants, has a heart as heavy as a lion, and a tongue that measures the distance of two soccer goal posts.

The fastest animal in the sea is the sailfish. It's almost as fast as a cheetah. This is very impressive, as water is harder to power through than air.

The cheetah is the fastest land animal. It can run up to 75 mph (120 kph).

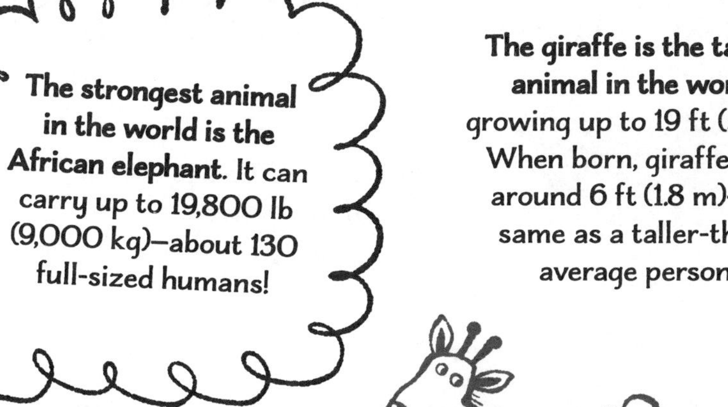

The strongest animal in the world is the African elephant. It can carry up to 19,800 lb (9,000 kg)—about 130 full-sized humans!

The giraffe is the tallest animal in the world, growing up to 19 ft (5.8 m). When born, giraffes are around 6 ft (1.8 m)—the same as a taller-than-average person.

The fastest animal in the air is the peregrine falcon. Its top speed is 242 mph (389 kmh) when it dives to hunt prey—speedier than sports cars! Peregrine falcons can also fly farther than the distance from the UK to Australia every year, to and from their nests!

Impressive ANIMALS

BEST SIGHT: Eagles can see **four times better** than the average human.

SUPER HEARING: Pigeons can hear incredibly **low frequency** sounds that humans can't, such as **volcanic eruptions.**

LONGEST TIME HOLDING BREATH: Cuvier's beaked whales can hold their breaths for over **three and a half hours.**

LOUDEST CLAWS: Pistol shrimps have one claw **larger** than the other. They can snap it shut so fast, that a **special bubble** is created, and when it bursts, it makes a sound louder than a **gunshot**, which **scares off predators and stuns prey.**

MOST SENSITIVE NOSES: Elephants. While dogs' noses are **1,000 to 10,000 times more sensitive** than ours, elephants' noses are **two times more sensitive** than that!

STRONGEST BITE: The saltwater crocodile's bite is 30 times stronger than ours, making it very **deadly**.

MOST VENOMOUS: Box jellyfish are very **dangerous** to humans and are named for their **cube-shaped** bodies.

It is believed that there are at least 8.7 million species on Earth, and 80 percent of these are still undiscovered!

Brilliant BIRDS

Birds are literally **dinosaurs**. Dinosaurs are defined as any animals that descended from the last common ancestor of two dinosaurs called Iguanodon and Megalosaurus, and this **includes birds!**

Flamingos aren't really pink. They're actually born gray, but their diet of shrimp and algae has a pink dye in it that turns their feathers pink.

Roosters crow as loudly as **chainsaws**. To stop themselves from going deaf, they **tilt their heads** back when they crow. This covers their ear canal, and acts like a **plug**.

Swifts can fly for almost a year **without landing**.

Vultures wee and poo on themselves to keep cool on hot days.

Hummingbirds are the only known birds that can fly **backward.**

The gray-headed albatross can fly **almost all the way around the world**. One albatross was recorded flying more than 13,670 miles (22,000 kilometers) around the Southern Hemisphere in **46 days**.

Ostriches lay the **biggest** eggs in the world. Each one is as big as 24 chicken eggs.

The color of a chicken's **earlobes** will usually predict the color of its eggs. A chicken with **dark** earlobes will lay **brown eggs** and a chicken with **white** earlobes will lay **white eggs**.

In **level flight**, the white-throated needletail is the **fastest bird in the air**, with a top speed of 105 mph (170 kph). This is as quick as a **high-speed train**!

Magnificent MAMMALS

In the same way that children suck their thumbs for comfort, baby elephants **suck their trunks.**

Koalas can sleep for up to **22 hours** a day. They have **fingerprints** that are almost identical to those of humans.

Giant anteaters consume up to **35,000** ants per day.

Duck-billed platypus don't have nipples, and feed their young by **sweating milk** out from special glands in their skin.

Otters hold hands when they sleep, so they don't float away.

One cow can poo up to 15 times per day, which is around 20 tons every year.

We can smell a skunk's spray up to **3.5 miles** away.

The edible dormouse can hibernate up to **11 months** per year.

Vampire bats **share blood** with their friends after a big meal.

Japanese macaques will play with **snowballs** for fun.

Amazing AMPHIBIANS

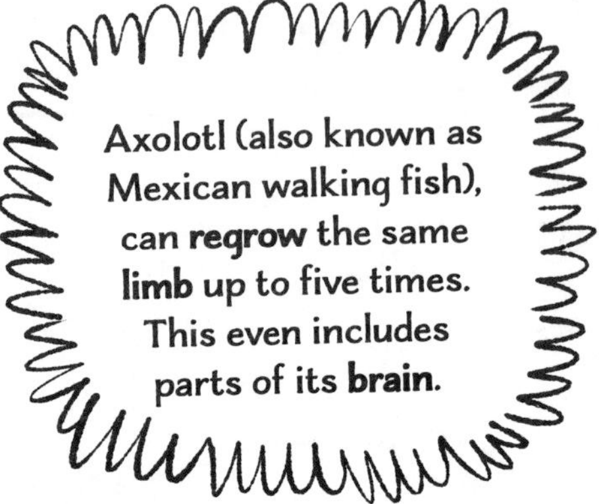

Axolotl (also known as Mexican walking fish), can **regrow** the same **limb** up to five times. This even includes parts of its **brain**.

The wood frog spends more than half of the year **frozen**, with its **heartbeat** and **blood flow** completely **stopped**.

The Chinese giant salamander is the **world's largest amphibian**. It can grow **longer than the height of an average man.**

Underground-dwelling caecilians may look like worms, but these are actually **amphibians who eat the skin of their own parents.**

The hairy frog, also known as the horror frog or wolverine frog, can **break its own bones** to produce **claws from its feet.**

Really Cool REPTILES

The Inland taipan is the most **venomous snake in the world** and has enough venom to kill **100** people with one bite.

To scare away predators, the horned lizard will inflate itself to **double** its size and can even **shoot blood from its eyes** up to a yard away.

The oldest known animal was named Adwaita. He was an **Aldabra giant tortoise**, born in 1750, that lived up to **255** years old.

Crocodiles carry their babies in their **mouths**.

The smallest reptile, the nano chameleon from Madagascar, is almost as small as the head of a **matchstick**.

Incredible INVERTEBRATES

The animal that causes the most human deaths is the **mosquito**. It carries diseases which kill more than **700,000** people each year.

The animal with the shortest adult lifespan is the **mayfly**. Though they only live as flying insects for **a few minutes** (or a few days maximum), baby mayflies can live **underwater** for several years as **nymphs** (their young form).

A cockroach can live for weeks after having its **head cut off**.

The **giant Pacific octopus** has **three hearts**, **nine brains**, and **blue blood**.

A garden snail's mouth is called a radula, and this can have more than 20,000 teeth.

Fleas can jump **200** times their body length.

There are over a billion insects for every human on Earth.

The **Dracula ant** has the fastest recorded animal movement on record. It can snap its jaw shut at **200 mph** (320 kph), in just 0.000015 seconds—that would be over 50,000 times in one second!

Bees have five eyes. Two at the front, and three smaller ones behind them.

Adult **rhinoceros beetles** can lift up to **850** times their own weight. This is the equivalent of a person lifting **ten** elephants.

Fascinating FISH

The female seahorse deposits her eggs inside the **male's pouch**, so it is the males who **carry their babies** until birth.

Great white sharks have a keen **sense of smell**, and can detect just one drop of **blood** in over **26 gallons** of water.

Snailfish are the deepest ocean dwellers on record, living around **26,000 ft (8,000 m) below the surface**—that's a similar height to the world's tallest mountain, Mount Everest.

LUNGFISH are the only fish with **lungs AND gills.**

Electric eels are not actually eels. They're more closely related to **catfish**.

Sunfish can lay up to **300 million** eggs throughout their lives. This is the **highest of any known animal.**

Archerfish **shoot** their prey! They **squirt jets of water** at insects to dislodge them from plants above the surface, so they fall into the water and can be eaten.

Whale sharks are by far the largest fish, and the biggest one ever caught was 62 ft (19 m) long. **thickest** of any known animal.

Mudskipper fish can **walk on land** and survive up to two days at a time out of the water.

Atlantic bluefin tuna can weigh as much as **2,000 lbs (900 kg)**–this is more than a horse.

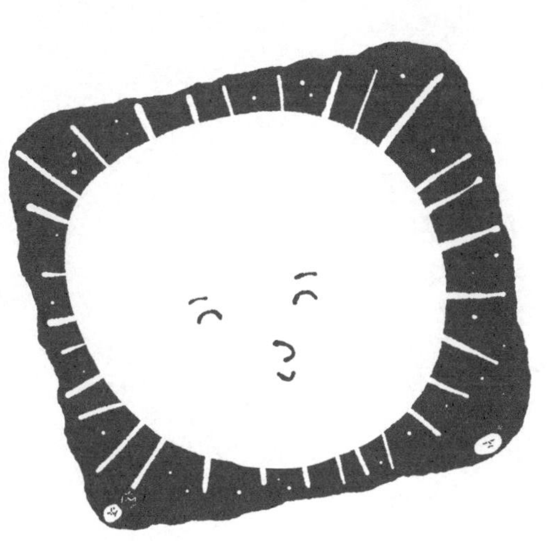

SCIENCE

The WHEEL

Invented by **Sumerian people in Mesopotamia**, the wheel is often considered the **most important invention in history**. However, the wheel's creation was more complicated than it sounds...

The TELEPHONE

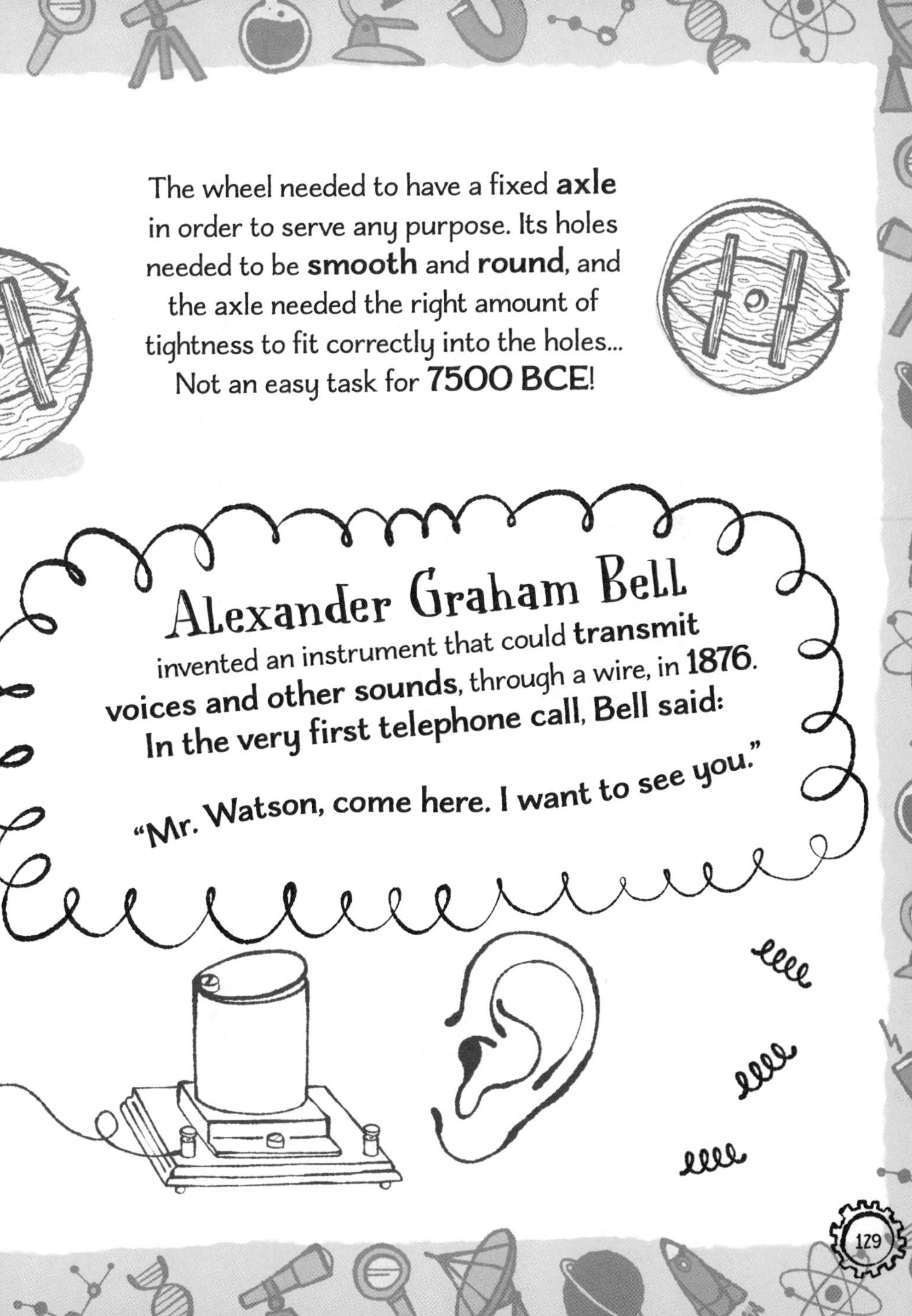

The wheel needed to have a fixed **axle** in order to serve any purpose. Its holes needed to be **smooth** and **round**, and the axle needed the right amount of tightness to fit correctly into the holes... Not an easy task for **7500 BCE**!

Alexander Graham Bell

invented an instrument that could **transmit voices and other sounds**, through a wire, in **1876**. **In the very first telephone call, Bell said:**

"Mr. Watson, come here. I want to see you."

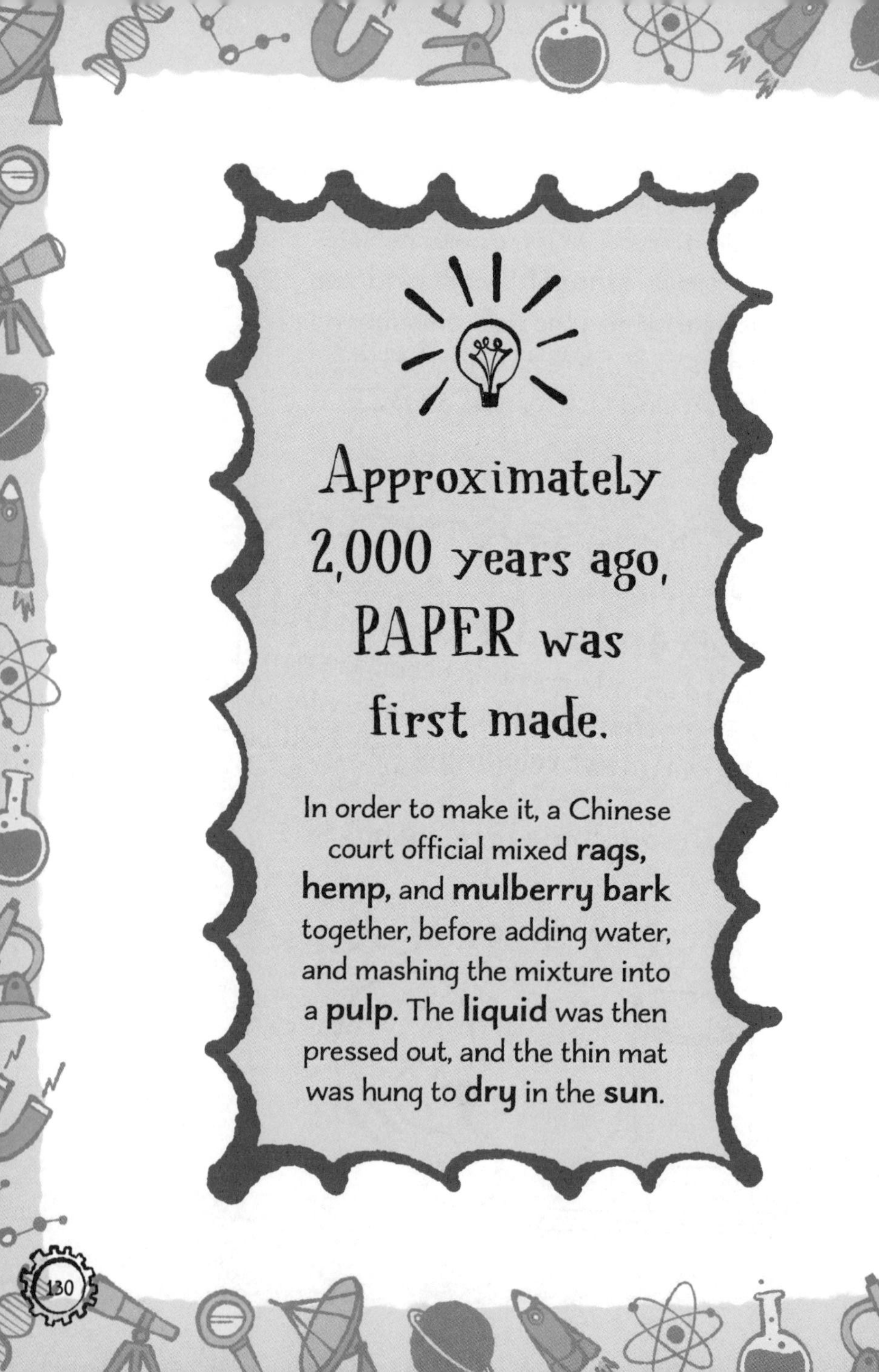

Approximately 2,000 years ago, PAPER was first made.

In order to make it, a Chinese court official mixed **rags, hemp,** and **mulberry bark** together, before adding water, and mashing the mixture into a **pulp**. The **liquid** was then pressed out, and the thin mat was hung to **dry** in the **sun**.

The COMPASS

A **compass** is one of the most important instruments for **navigation**.

The ends of the needle point to the magnetic **north** and magnetic **south**.

A **magnetic compass** consists of a **magnetized needle** that rotates, so it lines up with Earth's magnetic field.

The COMPASS was invented in China, between 200BCE and 100CE.

The PRINTING PRESS

The **oldest known printed text** was a Buddhist scroll made in China, using **block printing**.

However, in **1436, Johannes Gutenberg** created a **printing press,** using metal blocks for each letter. This enabled **200 copies of the Bible** to be printed within three years (which at that time was incredibly fast). The printing press changed the world. Books, pamphlets, and papers became affordable, and **many people then learned to read.**

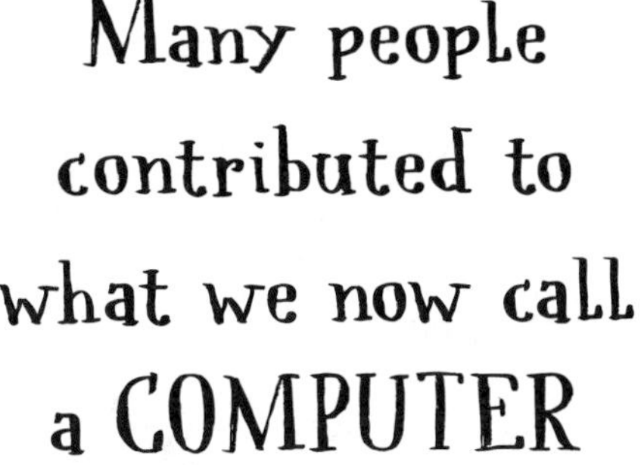

Many people contributed to what we now call a COMPUTER

The idea of an **automatic digital computer** dates back to mathematical prodigy **Charles Babbage**. He imagined the "**Analytical Engine,**" a device that could execute math operations and would include a memory unit.

In **1946**, scientists **John William Mauchly** and **J. Presper Eckert** created the first general-purpose computer—the Electronic Numerical Integrator and Computer **(ENIAC)**.

There were also huge contributions from six female programmers that were essential to the success of ENIAC.

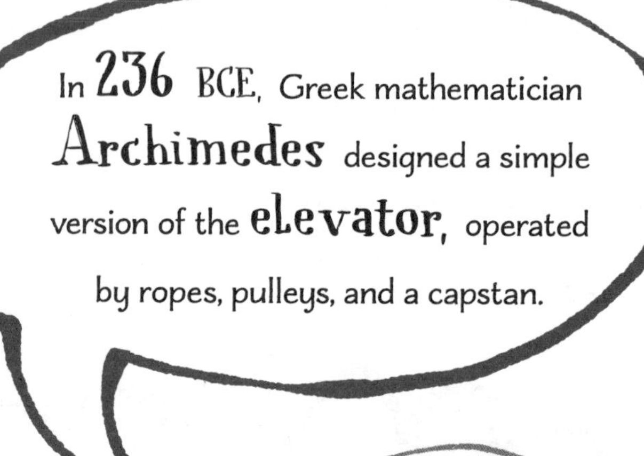

The modern ELEVATOR

as we know it was created in **1854**, when **Elisha Otis** created an elevator with a **safety hoist**. This safety hoist stopped people from falling if a chain or rope broke. The Otis company continues to make elevators today.

The LIGHT BULB was invented by Thomas Edison and a team of researchers

The first **light bulb**s were called "**incandescent**" light bulbs, meaning that the light was created by a very thin piece of metal (also known as a **filament**) inside the bulb. The electricity heated the wire, so it glowed with light.

After more than 3,000 different designs, Edison's team managed to invent a light bulb that was practical and not expensive.

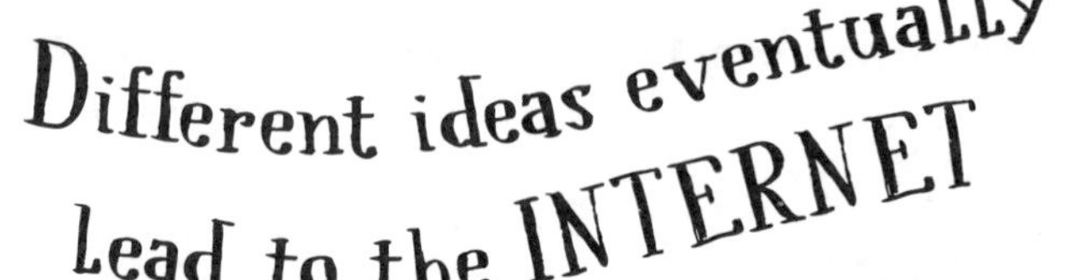

Different ideas eventually lead to the INTERNET

But arguably the most significant **invention**

to help create it was the

World Wide Web by Tim Berners Lee,

which included many of the

principles we use today.

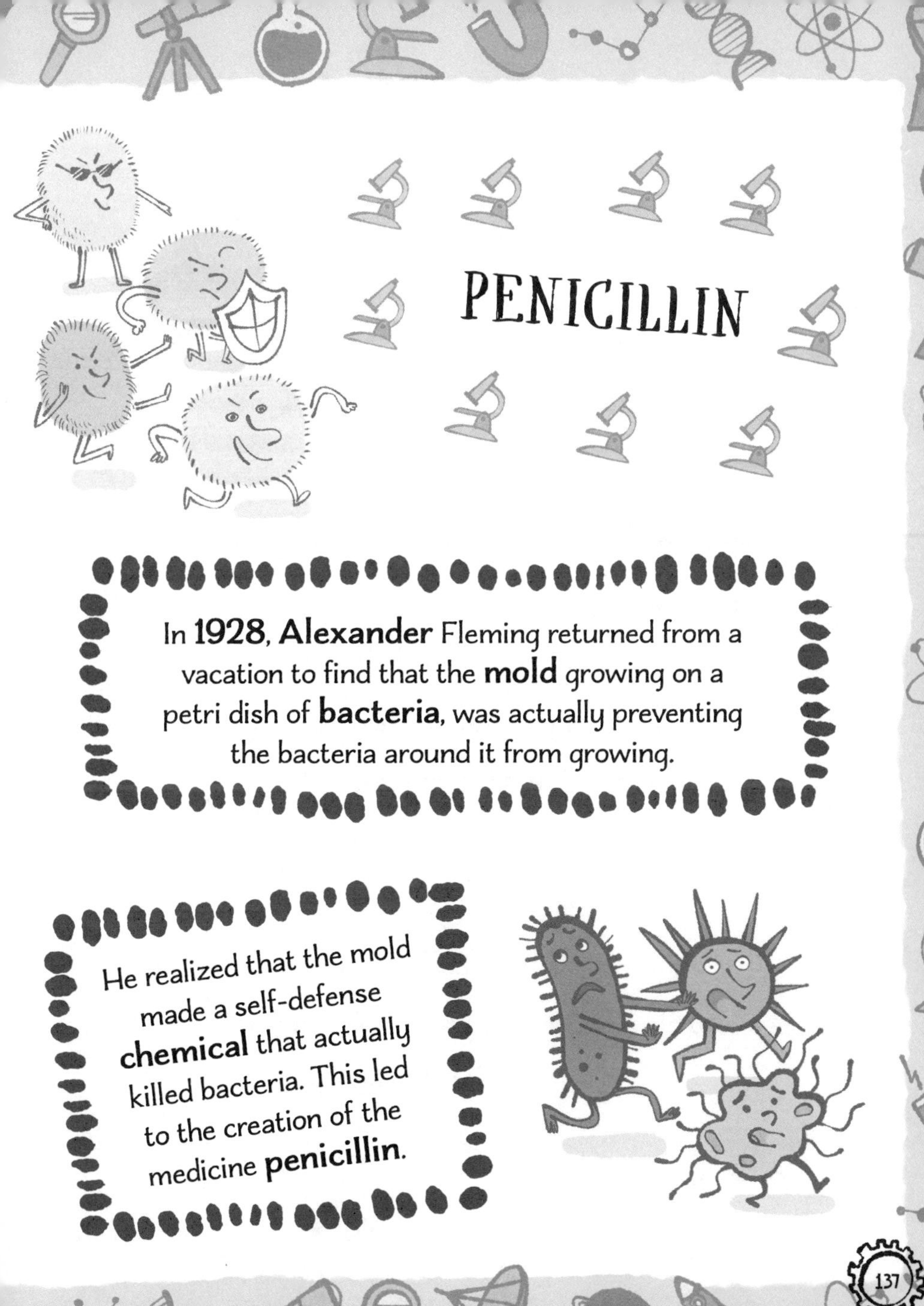

PENICILLIN

In **1928**, **Alexander** Fleming returned from a vacation to find that the **mold** growing on a petri dish of **bacteria**, was actually preventing the bacteria around it from growing.

He realized that the mold made a self-defense **chemical** that actually killed bacteria. This led to the creation of the medicine **penicillin**.

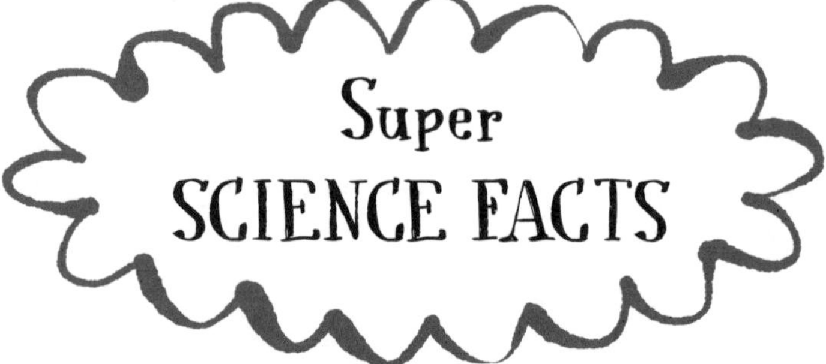

Super SCIENCE FACTS

Some **metals** EXPLODE if they come into contact with **water**. These include **potassium**, **sodium**, **lithium**, **rubidium**, and **cesium**. They are known as **reactive metals**.

When **uncoiled**, the DNA in a **person's body** would stretch the distance from Pluto to the Sun and back!

About **50 percent** of all the **natural history specimens** held in **museums** across the globe are incorrectly labeled, according to a study. Uh-oh, I guess you can't believe everything you read!

A **person's sneeze** can travel at speeds of about **100 miles per hour**.

Experts predict that there will be **9.7 billion people** on Earth by **2050**.

We often think of **clouds** as being **weightless**, but clouds can weigh around **1 million lbs (450,000 kg)**. That's about the same weight as the world's **largest jet** when it's completely **full of cargo and passengers**.

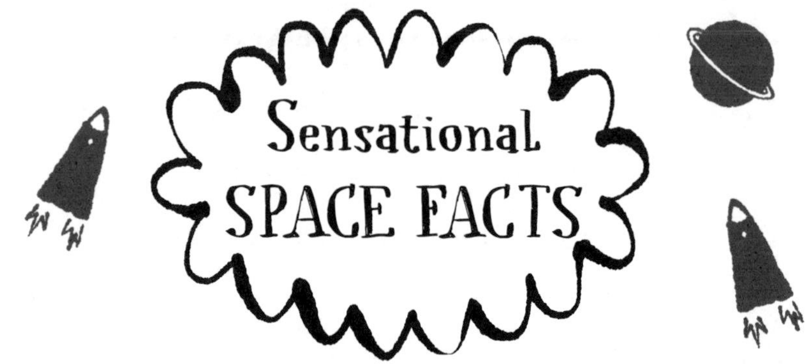

Sensational SPACE FACTS

Our **Sun** is an average-sized star, and **one million** planet **Earths** can fit inside it. Plus, the mass of our Sun takes up **99.86 percent** of our **solar system**!

The **Earth's core** is as hot as the surface of the **Sun**.

If you were able to **fly** a plane to the dwarf planet **Pluto**, it would take more than **800 years**!

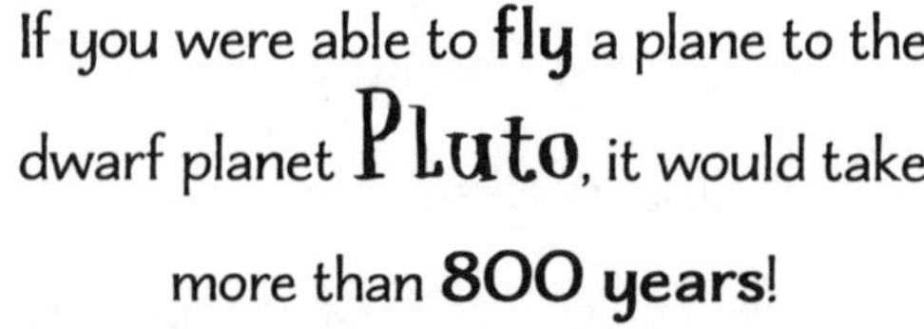

The **first animals in space** were **fruit flies**, which were sent up in **1947** and recovered **alive.**

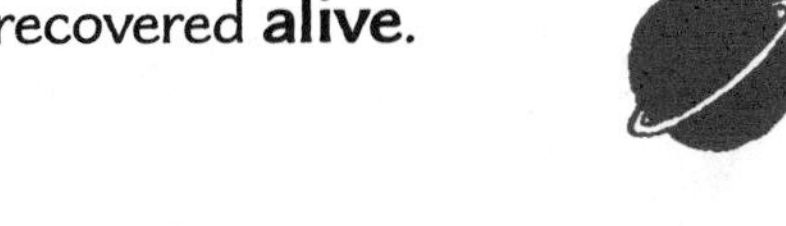

The **Apollo space program** was named after the **Greek god Apollo.** He is the **god** of **light, music, poetry, art, prophecy, truth**, and more!

Because the **gravity** in **outer space** is so low, **astronauts** can't **burp!** The **liquid** and **gases** in their stomach cannot separate.

It is completely **silent** in **space** as there is no way for **sound** to travel.

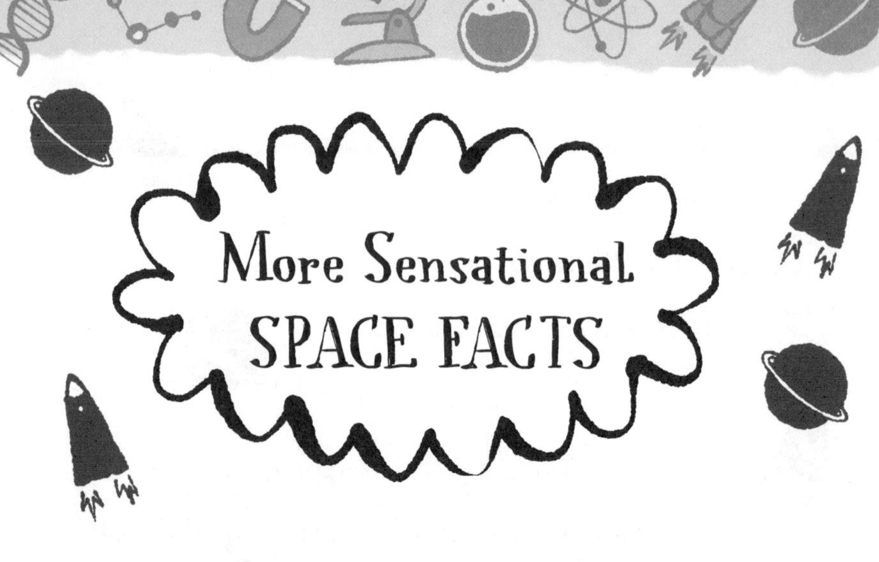

There were **footprints** and **tire tracks** left on the **moon** by **astronauts**, and these will be there forever as there is **no wind to blow them away**.

If you were on the planet **Mars**, **sunsets** would appear **blue**.

There is actual **junk in space** floating around! Scientists estimate there are about **500,000 pieces** of space junk in space today.

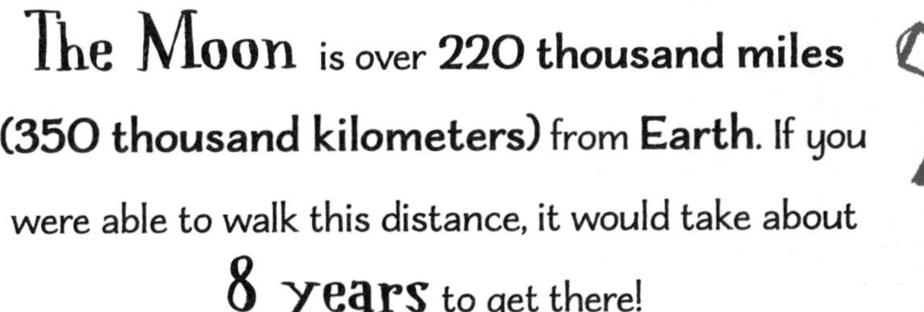

The Moon is over **220 thousand miles (350 thousand kilometers)** from **Earth**. If you were able to walk this distance, it would take about **8 years** to get there!

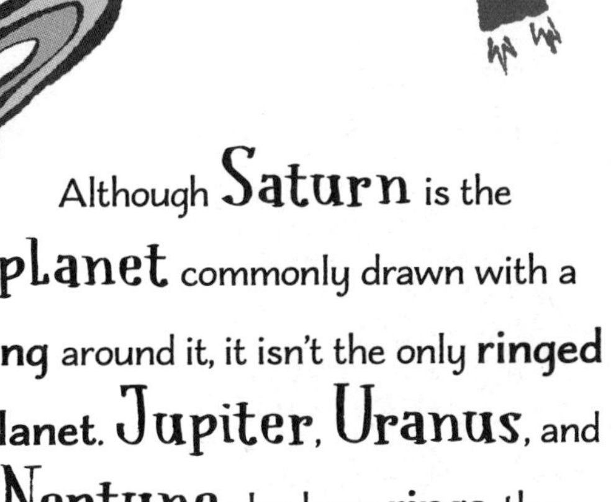

Although **Saturn** is the **planet** commonly drawn with a **ring** around it, it isn't the only **ringed** planet. **Jupiter**, **Uranus**, and **Neptune** also have **rings**, they are just less visible.

A full **NASA** space suit costs approximately **$150 million** (£117 million)!

About the author

Radzi is one of Britain's most talented and experienced television presenters, having started out his presenting career on the BBC's landmark children's show, Blue Peter. He has since gone on to be a regular face on our screens, presenting shows for the BBC, ITV, Channel 4, Amazon, and Eurosport. Radzi is a highly knowledgeable sports presenter, reporting across the Olympics, Paralympics, athletics, tennis, Formula E, and basketball. As one of TNT Eurosport's leading presenters, Radzi traveled the world filming "Road To Beijing" ahead of the Winter Olympics, where he reported live from China as well as hosting the channel's Snooker coverage. And he will be anchoring the channel's coverage of the Paris Olympics in 2024. Radzi also works across the factual space, presenting programs such as Songs of Praise and Crufts, as well as appearing in entertainment shows such as Dancing on Ice, Beat The Chasers, Supermarket Sweep, and All Star Musicals at Christmas. He is the author of DK's Move Like a Lion (2021) and Move Like A Cub (2023).

You can follow him on Twitter, Instagram, and TikTok at @iamradzi.

Acknowledgments:

Growing up I went to six different schools, so I'd like to thank the many brilliant teachers I had. A special thanks to the Adams' Grammar School, and in particular to Mr. Thompson, Mr. Chapman, Mr. Warren-Smith, Mr. Hunt, and Mr. Banks for epitomizing what a teacher is.

Thank you to my team: Alex, Maddy, and DK for helping to make this book possible. Eternal thanks to my Mum (Barbara) and Sister (Rufaro) for endless love, support, and belief. And thank you to you—the reader—for choosing my book: it means more than you know.

DK would like to thank:

Lol Johnson for the cover photograph. Alex Fisher and Madison Lygo from M&C Saatchi Merlin. Elizabeth Counsell, and Hannah Weatherill from Northbank Talent.

The publisher would like to thank the following for their kind permission to reproduce their photographs:

Cover images: *Front:* **iStock:** Enjoynz c; CSA-Printstock c. *Back:* **iStock:** Enjoynz c; CSA-Printstock c. *Spine:* **iStock:** Enjoynz c; CSA-Printstock c.